TEMPUS
Oral History
SERIES

HEADINGLEY
RUGBY
voices

DAILY SKETCH

SATURDAY, SEPTEMBER 19, 1931. Head Office, 200, Gray's Inn-road, W.C.1. 'Phone: Museum 5841.

Dance the Tango by Wireless To-night: See Page 13

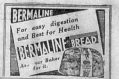
LEEDS MEN WHO WILL FIGHT FOR RUGBY HONOURS

A special *Daily Sketch* page of action pictures of Leeds, one of the most prominent Yorkshire members of the Rugby League. Above are some of the team.

Joe Thompson, English International and the team's goal-kicker.

R. J. Welch, an International forward, with Mr. Bright Heyhurst, the trainer of the team.

J. Cox, second line forward.

J. Busch, half-back and Australian International.

D. Jenkins, second row forward.

Jimmy Douglas, second line forward.

Thomas, a forward, who is leaving the club to play for York.

Leslie Adams, half-back and English International.

F. O'Rourke, centre three-quarter and Australian International, and Stanley Smith, wing three-quarter and International.

Members of the forward line practising a passing movement.

Printed and Published for the DAILY SKETCH AND SUNDAY GRAPHIC, LTD., 200, Gray's Inn-road, London, W.C.1, by ALLIED NEWSPAPERS LIMITED, Withy Grove, Manchester.—SATURDAY, SEPTEMBER 19, 1931.

2

TEMPUS
Oral History
SERIES

HEADINGLEY
RUGBY
voices

Compiled by
Phil Caplan

TEMPUS

First published 1999
Copyright © Phil Caplan, 1999

Tempus Publishing Limited
The Mill, Brimscombe Port,
Stroud, Gloucestershire, GL5 2QG

ISBN 0 7524 1822 X

Typesetting and origination by
Tempus Publishing Limited
Printed in Great Britain by
Midway Clark Printing, Wiltshire

LEEDS R. L
CLUB

SUPPORTERS
HANDBOOK
1968 - 1969
1/6

1967-68 HONOURS LIST
R.L. Cup Winners
League Leaders
Yorks. League Champions
Mackeson Trophy Winners
Yorks. Senior Comp. Champion
Yorks. Senior Cup Winners

"THE MOST IMPORTANT TRY IN 45 YEARS" — see page 24

CONTENTS

Foreword by Graham Murray   6

Introduction   7

Acknowledgements   9

1.   Earliest Recollections   11

2.   Getting to the Game   26

3.   Debuts and Great Players   36

4.   Rituals and Superstitions   52

5.   The Magic and Despair of the Cup   61

6.   Headingley is Home   79

7.   Away Days   93

8.   Laughter and Tears   111

FOREWORD

Two things struck me soon after I arrived in early 1998, the passion and knowledge of the Leeds fans and the magic of Headingley. Essentially the two go hand in hand and over the two years I have been here we have had some wonderful nights at the famous old stadium. The players will always give their all but their efforts seem to reach a greater level and have more meaning if they are willed on and appreciated by the fans.

I have felt very proud and privileged to be able to bring some success to the supporters during my reign. The expectation was intense but so was the patience and the win at Wembley, in particular, was as much for them as it was the players and coaches to savour. For that reason alone the Headingley homecoming on the Sunday after the final was extra special.

I've always been a student of the history of the game and one of the reasons I was so keen to come to Leeds was the lure of Headingley. It has so many associations with the greats of the code and means as much to Australians as it does to those who have grown up with it. From the minute I set foot in the ground I knew that this place was something really special, like the old Sydney Cricket Ground.

I am delighted that a book has been written to commemorate what Headingley means to Leeds fans and that recognition has been given to the sacrifices and part that they play in making it what it is. I enjoy any good yarn about the game we all love and there are plenty in here – both poignant and humorous. What keeps coming through is that we are all part of the same family and I am just delighted to have played some small part in it.

Graham Murray
Head coach, Leeds Rhinos 1998-99

Modern professional sport has seen a significant shift away from the supporter: the fan has become a consumer and the match a product. Once commercial forces – particularly television revenue – became more valuable than the pound through the gate that shift was inevitable and inexorable. Nevertheless, if any code has managed to maintain its links with those whose loyalty knows no bounds, then it is Rugby League. Economic pressures do inevitably dictate, but the sense of community, of shared emotion between passionate followers and accessible heroes, sets the thirteen-a-side game apart.

At about the time the idea of *Headingley Rugby Voices* began to become reality, the Rugby Football League unveiled a new slogan to brand and market the sport for the next millennium. They chose 'Love this game' and that phrase epitomises why so many people were eager to offer their time, contributions and support for this book. Whatever our allegiances and however bitter the rivalries, which are heightened when the fixture calendar contains so many local derbies, the supporters have always been fiercely proud and protective of the pastime that they were instrumental in nurturing and developing in the face of prejudice and open hostility. Their attendance in the crucial early years when the Northern Union voted to recompense players for broken time loss of earnings ensured that the venture would succeed. As a corollary, rules were changed and adapted to ensure displays of the kind of skills that would attract a paying public. That ethos is still evident today and in part accounts for the feeling that 'we are all in this together' which is such a distinguishing feature of Rugby League.

There has rarely, if ever, been a book about the game that commemorates occasions and contentions solely from the fans' perspective. What is really important to them and why, the lengths they will go (both literally and metaphorically) to follow their chosen side, the anecdotes and exaggerations that are integral to donning the club colours with such pride. A conscious decision was taken when compiling the material to avoid courting the views or corroborations of players and officials for that very reason. There may be factual errors amongst the tales and recollections – dates, times and the players involved may be wrong – but if this is how events are treasured and cherished then who are we to interfere with precious and often long-held memories. The *raison d'être* of this book was to get behind the actuality and into the emotion and true feeling, the common bond that binds together the fans of Leeds with the majesty of Headingley – irrespective of whether they were Loiners or are now Rhinos.

There are historic contradictions that are an integral part of being a Leeds fan. The old adage that 'a strong Leeds is good for the game' is balanced by the fact that there is an overwhelming desire amongst the majority of other clubs to see them beaten. Part of that is due to the fact that Headingley has always been revered as being the best bespoke facilities in the game and that opposition players and fans love nothing better than to overturn the 'aristocrats', especially on their own midden. Historically, the unique green sward in Leeds 6 has been synonymous with entertaining, flowing rugby characterised by flashing touchline dashes and inventive half back play. It has often been said that the fans of the blue and amber would be happier seeing their side lose 28-30 than win 2-0, which is possibly why Leeds have been a more successful in cup competitions rather than exhibiting the kind of dogged consistency needed to claim Championship titles. It is the promise of a brand of free-flowing rugby that has kept the fan base loyal when in terms of the talent assembled there have been periods of underachievement.

This collection of reminiscences, tales and evangelism attempts to explain why the thrill of expectation is often a greater pull than the glory that occasionally comes with it. How an early recollection ensured a lifelong attachment, the sacrifices fans will make to see their heroes in action, the cherished warmth remembering the deeds of the greats, the almost ceremonial traditions of support culminating in moments of excruciating despair or unbounded ecstasy, all for the cause. Being a true fan is a terminal disease no matter which club or sport you follow, the involvement is total and at times overwhelming. There is also a collective camaraderie and shared emotion that few other facets of life can offer, which is why it is so important. Hopefully some of that passion is represented here, after all the best action photographs of sporting events are framed by the reaction of the crowd in the background. Announcing the latest redevelopment programme for Headingley in May 1999 which will see the famous South Stand terracing given an upgrade and facelift, officials from the Leeds board commented, 'We are proud of the fans who combine Rugby League knowledge with loyalty and humour. They play a major role with their inspirational vocal backing'. It is hoped that this book is a small reflection of that sentiment.

Phil Caplan
June 1999

ACKNOWLEDGEMENTS

So many people gave their time and backing readily and willingly in an effort to support this venture, whether it be a passing comment or anecdote or by providing unstinting hospitality and patience in their homes. Essentially we just spent some time sharing a passion and hopefully they enjoyed talking about the greatest game as much as I did. Their names are included under each (much-appreciated) contribution and I hope the transcription and context does justice to their rich seam of reminiscence. In terms of photographs and associated memorabilia, the support of Dave Williams was invaluable as were the collections of John Walker, from his Uncle Joe, and the family of Eric Rosenhead – one of the staunchest Leeds fans ever. Access to the Headingley archive and continual encouragement from Phil Daly at the club was also a great help. Thanks also to Ros for lining up potential interviewees and reading the proofs.

This book is dedicated to two of the finest players and gentlemen ever to don the blue and amber, Arthur Clues and Roy Powell, who sadly passed away in 1998 but whose memories will be cherished forever by their respective generations.

THE MICK SHOEBOTTOM TESTIMONIAL FUND

LEEDS v GT. BRITAIN

TUESDAY, 11th JANUARY, 1972 - 7-30 p.m.

SOUVENIR PROGRAMME 10p

CHAPTER 1

Earliest Recollections

Preparing for the season that brought the cup to Headingley.

Mr Sewell read letter he had received from Mr Holdsworth saying that a meeting would be held at the Mitre Hotel on Tuesday, the 27th inst at 7.30 for the purpose of forming a Northern Union & taking definite action. After a long discussion Mr Penney pro. and Mr Oldham sec.

"That our representatives be empowered to support a resolution for the formation of a Northern Rugby Union if in their opinion the majority of the Clubs are in favour of it."

Carried by 15 votes to 2.

Mr Miller & Mr Brown voted against. Mr Miller then resigned his position as President and left the room. Mr Brown also resigned but subsequently withdrew his resignation. Mr Penney was voted to the Chair.

Messrs. Sewell & Connell were appointed as the representatives of the Club at the meeting in question.

E. Smith pro. & G. Fowler sec. "That the representatives be empowered to take immediate steps to resign the membership of the Rugby Union should the majority decide to do so. (Carried)

Resolved that the resignation of the Club be prepared and signed by the Hon: Sec: in readiness for any emergency which may arise."

Minutes from the most historic committee meeting in the club's history – the mandate to break away in 1895.

12

A Family Thing

Rugby League was always something I did with my grandfather. He lived right next door to Headingley and their garden backed on to the ginnel that ran up to the cricket ground. I used to spend every Saturday with them because my parents were working. Mornings were with my grandma doing baking, shopping and girlie things and in the afternoon it was boys' things because I was the only grandchild, which meant going to the match. I was about seven at the time and it was during the mid-sixties when Leeds had a great side containing the likes of Bev Risman and John Atkinson – who was my hero when I was a kid. Everyone in the family used to go at some time, even my mum, and my dad was a bit of an expert as he used to play, so we were always talking about the game. We often met cousins or other relatives at Headingley and whenever there was a family occasion talk always used to centre on the fortunes of Leeds Rugby. We still send videos out to places like Hong Kong for those amongst us who can't get to see them play. We always stood behind the goals at the Western End, opposite to where the players used to run out from the corner of the old pavilion, and we were frequently joined by my grandfather's brother. Somehow we were all in it together. I never minded going but I also knew that if I got bored I could always run back round to my grandma's and the same was true of the cricket in the summer. I've just grown up with Headingley and Leeds always being there. Leading up to Wembley this year [1999] we were talking about it at work and my boss said, 'Oh, I expect you're just going because it's the final', and I got quite indignant with him and left him in no doubt just how deep-seated my passion for the club is. Nowadays, appearances might be deceptive but I couldn't support anybody else even if I wanted to!

Sue Munden

A Good Start

The first game I ever went to was Leeds *v.* Wakefield in 1987 when we won pretty easily. From the kick-off Andrew Ettingshausen caught the ball and went straight up the South Stand side and almost the length of the field before drawing the cover and putting Phil Fox striding in at the corner. That left an immediate impression on me! My second match was about a year later, again on a free ticket from Westfield Junior School, against Castleford when we won 44-0 this time. I thought big Headingley victories were just the norm.

Andrew Jagger

No Option

I was born on a match day so it's hardly surprising that I grew up as a fanatic. It was an Easter Saturday and that afternoon Leeds played Hunslet in the traditional derby fixture at Headingley, kicking off twelve hours after I had made my debut at the nursing home. Years later I asked my Dad if he went to the game. His reply was short and to the point, 'What do you think?'. Apparently we won 4-0.

Howard Brooks

May 24
1901

Eleventh Annual General Meeting held at the Pavilion, Mr Sheldon in the Chair. Members present 153.

at meeting were o were read

The Leeds Cricket, Football, and Athletic Co.

LIMITED.

r. M. W. Nicholson it was resolved went of Accounts

THE LEEDS
RUGBY FOOTBALL CLUB.

rt + Statement be adopted (Carried)

RULES.

1.—The Club shall be called "THE LEEDS RUGBY FOOTBALL CLUB," and shall be a member of the Northern Rugby Football Union, and shall be subject to the Bye-Laws of the Company.

lowing portion deleted

2.—The name of any person desiring to become a Member of the Club must be submitted to the Committee for approval.

3.—The Club shall be governed by a Committee, which shall consist of a President and eight others, to be elected at the Annual General Meeting, all of whom must be Full Members of the Company. The Hon. Secretary shall be elected by the Committee. The Captains of the 1st and 2nd Teams shall be elected by the Committee, and only have seats on the Committee during the selection of the Teams. The Secretary of the Leeds Cricket, Football, and Athletic Company, Limited, shall be ex-officio a member of the Committee. Four shall form a quorum. The Committee shall have power to fill any vacancy which may occur. Nominations for President and Committee shall be made in writing to the Secretary, duly proposed and seconded, seven clear days prior to the date of the General Meeting, to be held in May, of which fourteen days' notice shall be given in *The Leeds and Yorkshire Mercury* and *The Yorkshire Post*. Each person nominated must have given his consent before his nomination is sent in.

nittee, t eight eneral elected nall be le for all be e first ighest rs, and of the ear in ection. either

substituted :—

nittee, Hon. elected

Mr Waring pro.) as an amendment That the Club Walmsley sec.) shall be governed by a Committee.

The first codified set of rules for the new Leeds CF&A club drawn up for the 1901/02 season.

14

A team shot from September 1921, taken prior to defeating Wakefield at Headingley. This side went on to lift the Yorkshire Cup.

Northern Union Beginnings

I got interested in following Rugby League through going to Bus Vale in the early twenties to see amateur matches. From there we moved up the road to Headingley to watch Leeds play in what was still the Northern Union. The rules were very primitive compared to today but there were wonderful players and characters like Joe Thompson and Jeff Moores, who we were in awe of. They were all extremely fit considering the full-time jobs they had and the lack of training facilities. The same was true of the trainers, whose techniques were very basic because they worked through the day as well – they didn't even get to pick the team. By the thirties Leeds had gathered an exceptional side together that played some spectacular rugby. The game attracted us because we didn't know anything else: soccer was always second place, it was rugby or nothing. We still went to Bus Vale on Sunday mornings to keep the interest going, especially as some of our friends and contemporaries turned out and professional scouts used to come and watch them. One, called Maurice Bush, whose career we followed and supported went on to sign for Bramley.

Oscar Caplan

Two Daunting Prospects

During the 1950s we always used to go the game by car – a Vauxhall, which was relatively rare in those days,

15

Glorious cup winners – from left to right, standing: Ashton, Jackson, Dixon, Davis, Trusler, Thompson, Morn (trainer). Middle row: Bowen, Walmsley, Bacon, Lyons, Buck. Front row: Brittain, Binks.

because my dad was always a traveller. We used to find a parking space in one of the back streets, which everybody still does, and make our way to a sweet shop on the corner of Kirkstall Lane which was owned by an ex-player. I can't remember his name but I know that I was in awe of him. We always went in there to buy our half-time snacks which added to the feeling of match day being a real treat. Then came the two horrific moments for an impressionable young child. We used to gain admittance to the cricket ground first through the large gateway and it was separate turnstiles for men and boys in those days. I went through the boys'

entrance with my own bit of money and I used to have terrifying visions wondering what would I do if my dad wasn't there on the other side waiting for me. After coping with that, we used to transfer to the seats – we never stood, which is interesting because my children now when we go anywhere only ever want to stand – which meant another set of turnstiles. Because I was small, I was one of those who was lifted over and I hated it because I was always convinced that I was going to fall or trip or be dropped. Then there was the problem of not being able to see properly, first because there was usually a dirty great iron girder in the way obscuring the try-line and second, being only an eight or nine year old below average height, when everybody else stood up – because say Wilf Rosenberg the flying dentist from South Africa was on the charge – all I saw were coats in front of me. I've probably not seen some of the finest tries ever scored at Headingley! There was an occasion coming out of the ground after St Helens had thrashed us and it was all quiet that I uttered the immortal words 'Who won?' because I hadn't seen a damn thing.

Stuart Charmak

All in the Family

My late father was a local amateur referee, so the whole family is steeped in Rugby League tradition. He started bringing me to matches when I was three or four years old, just after the war, and I can still recall playing about on the little paddock that used to be in the front of the stadium. We were totally fascinated by a place that catered for two sports at the same time and at the beginning of the rugby season you used to come along and find a match on both sides of the ground. One Saturday we all rushed over from the rugby side to watch Freddie Trueman come in to bat and he was out first ball. As a treat, we were allowed to stay on that evening to watch him bowl. You got a season ticket book in those days that entitled

Joe Thompson, the Leeds crack goal-kicker, getting ready for the Rugby League Championship tussle in May 1929. Leeds lost by the narrowest of margins.

1931 BRAVO, LEEDS!

YORKS. CHAMPIONS

JEFF MOORES
with the Yorkshire Rugby League
Cup which Leeds, of whom he is
captain, have won by defeating
Dewsbury.

Australian pin-up and mentor to Eric Harris.

Baptism of Fire

Strangely enough, the first match I went to was an away game, standing on the stone and shale at Belle Vue in 1945 as competitive rugby resumed after the war. All the sides were in a period of transition but that afternoon Leeds were beaten 71-0! We weren't too upset or scarred because it was such a novelty and sense of occasion to see a live game. Even the travel to and from the grounds in those days, whether by bus, tram or train, was all just part of the entertainment. One Good Friday evening I had to walk all the way from Stanningley to Headingley to see the derby match against Bramley because there was a bus strike and never even thought twice about it. People's expectations were very low after the war, they were only too happy to be able to go out and watch and be part of sport. The atmosphere in the grounds was terrific, especially as crowds of 30,000 or more were commonplace. There was never any trouble, children were passed down over the heads of the adults to sit on the walls at the front and going to the game was an absolute pleasure. Working people lived from one match to the other and made every effort to get to see the action, no matter how much inconvenience there was getting there. We always travelled in fear to Lancashire as we went through an era when good hidings over there were the norm. Of course the odd victories then stood out from the expected defeat but the result never put anyone off going to support their team, whatever was happening to them. Winning wasn't everything, going was the important thing and it

you to do the cricket and rugby. For home games we used to catch the old forty-four bus from Harehills, but if we went via town we used get the number one tram to the ground. Things have changed, but in those days the stadium was ringed by lines and lines of public transport. It was a different sort of congestion to nowadays.

Mel Reuben

18

became a way of life that we took very seriously.

Geoff Caplan

In the Genes

My devotion to Leeds comes from my family, especially my grandmother who was secretary of the RFL for thirty-five years, her husband and my dad – who has followed the team for most of his life. I've always felt something passionate for this team because I have been brought up through it. My first match was when I was two, I came to Headingley on 1 January 1982 when Leeds played Oldham. I sat in the middle of the main stand and in the run-up to the game I ran on the pitch and shouted, 'I want to play with the big boys'. At half-time my dad drove me home, threw me through the front door and was back before the restart. I was an absolute nuisance but the love affair had begun. It probably started even before that because my grandpa had a Leeds shirt made for me even before I was born.

Marc Grant

Initially a Substitute

I first started supporting Leeds in my late teens when my brother went away to college. Until then I had not really been encouraged to go to matches, despite wanting to travel to Wembley in 1977. I was told that it wasn't really a girl's thing! I thought

Stan Smith, the fastest man on the Leeds books during the glorious '30s, was a supreme winger.

going instead of him would be a bit of a chore because I had to send a long letter including a full match report, the programme and all the cuttings to Coventry straight afterwards on the Monday morning, but I became a passionate fanatic overnight in my own right. I used to stand with the same crowd in the paddock and gradually we got to know the players socially which added to the enjoyment.

Tracey Collins

Bringing It All Back

When the Rhinos brought back the Challenge Cup for the homecoming at Headingley this season, I suddenly recalled a story my dad had told me, as I waited for the present day players to come out onto the pitch. After Leeds had first won at Wembley in 1936 they loaned the cup out to local businesses so the fans could see it in all its glory and it used to rest on display in shop windows around the area. Near where my dad lived, it sat proudly in the butchers for a while and he used to sprint home from school every afternoon just so that he could have a look in at the coveted silverware. Soon afterwards, the butcher invited him in not only to touch the trophy but also allowed him to have a drink out of it. Because he was only a child there was no chance of it being anything alcoholic to commemorate the historic victory, so he had to settle for dandelion and burdock.

Ken Fawcett

LOOKING AT DADDY'S CAPS.

'Jimmy' Brough, the Leeds Rugby League international full-back, with his wife and their ten-week-old son, Sammy, on 23 May 1933.

Some great players, including Arthur Clues (fourth from the right) and Lewis Jones (fifth from the right), who were recalled by many as the best of their generation.

An Interloper

My initial opinion of Rugby League was tainted because I come from the South. Until 1979, when I met Sue, I had this vision from the television of it always raining, there never being any grass on the pitch and it being difficult to tell the teams apart because they were always covered in mud. I came to Leeds and for the first match I went to at Headingley it was drizzling then, all of a sudden, Steve Pitchford ran out and it all seemed to fit the Eddie Waring type of image. At first, because I wasn't used to the flow of the game I thought it was really slow but it didn't take me long to realise that the players were always on the go and the fans' involvement total. Certainly sampling the game first hand changed my opinion of it completely.

Jim Munden

Winter

At the time of the big switch to summer with the advent of Super League, I thought that the game would be irrevocably changed. I guess I wasn't

21

JOHN ATKINSON

TESTIMONIAL YEAR
SOUVENIR
BROCHURE
1976

15

PRICE
20p

One of the finest finishers of the modern era – a true South Stand hero.

A case of divided loyalties – early recollections shape future allegiances.

The next generation learns that Friday night is Rhino night.

really in favour of the move because I hadn't known any different and all my habits and rituals centred around the winter months. Looking back now I realise that the only thing I miss is that indescribable feeling of rushing back from Headingley to get warm in front of the fire and drinking soup or hot chocolate as we mulled over the game and felt our toes and knees tingling and coming back to life. Because we had suffered hardship on the terraces battling the biting wind or the driving rain, we felt that we had played a part in the afternoon's efforts. It wasn't only the players that had been put out, we had made our sacrifice and contribution alongside them. My mum, or whoever,

would always have the kettle or saucepan on, waiting for our arrival like we had been on some Arctic expedition and the coats were dumped in the hall in the rush to get to the waiting mugs.

Gary Morrell

Lasting Impression

There might be many reasons why people go and see Rugby League and Leeds in particular. It can be a family thing carrying on a tradition or because they live near the ground or maybe they've got free time on a match day and are curious. Whatever, it's like a bug and you fall in love with the game and the team and the surroundings. Once you're bitten that's it, you might not go for a very long time but you retain this strong allegiance and fierce bond that you are always prepared to stand up for in any discussion anywhere in the world. Part of that feeling is a real and genuine pride in Headingley and what it stands for. You only need to see Leeds in action there once and you are smitten for life. It's a badge of identity, you might not go but you never go away.

Steve Marshall

Training Nights

The experience of match day – especially big ones at Headingley – is what you wait all week for, but you are part of a big crowd. When I first got into watching Leeds, the real fascination was turning up on cold winter nights to watch them train. It was somehow much more personal because if you were lucky you were one of a handful of sad die-hards and once you had been a few times the players used to recognise you and stop for a chat or a joke. That was when you felt like you really knew them and were a part of things. They used to train on that scrap of land behind the supporters' club in the South Stand car park and we used to watch either from the gate that led onto the field or looking over the wall from above at the back corner of the Western terrace. It was always freezing and the lighting was really poor when we arrived and all you could hear was the clatter of studs getting louder as the players jogged round the terracing to get to the pitch – for some

that was all they ever did. The best night to go was Thursday because you could learn a lot about team selection in those unsophisticated days. The squad usually split into two, the first and the 'A' team so you knew who had been dropped or promoted. Anyone who was injured just tended to do laps round the field and it was pretty easy to tell if they would be fit to play at the weekend. Occasionally we used to stand inside the fence near the one set of posts that was there and chase after balls if some of the goalkickers were practising. Virtually everybody could drop-kick and, although they might not have been accurate, some of the big forwards had tremendous boots on them and would send the ball spiralling into the gloom and we would chase them like faithful retrievers. We didn't learn much about tactics but it was always great to go into school on Friday morning and be able to predict pretty accurately what the team would be for the following day. After training we usually followed the players as they trotted back round to the old dressing rooms and they signed autographs or just chatted about things happening in the game. It's true that they are probably the last to know or be told things because they were always surprised at the gossip we had picked up from fans at other clubs. There was always a big urn of soup waiting for them in the recesses below the kitchens and many would sit and chat in there before having their bath. If it was really cold – or particularly disgusting – we even used to get offered a cup.

Benjamin Scott

CHAPTER 2

Getting to the Game

Marc Grant – some devotion knows no bounds!

Before Cars

In the 1930s we used to take a tram to the game. We lived in Hamilton Avenue and got the tram from Chapeltown right round town before changing for the journey to Headingley. We got off at Hyde Park corner and then walked to the stadium. What might now be seen as inconvenience was taken for granted because the only alternative was to walk all the way there – which we did when necessary if we only had enough money to get into the ground. We walked in crowds and used to meet our friends at a cafe in North Street called Jack Reeds and do the journey together. We always got the green *Sports Post* on the way home from the match in town on the Saturday night and that afternoon's report would already be in there, which was amazing really. What was special was the match itself, getting there – though enjoyable – was just the means to an end.

Oscar Caplan

From Two Wheels to Four

Occasionally I used to travel with my father to away matches after the war and as we had a tandem at the time we used to go on that. We went to Bradford to see Leeds play Northern at Odsal and chained the tandem to the railings outside, watched the game and then cycled back home. We thought nothing of it, being at the match was all that mattered. Getting to the game was all part of the adventure and when we all met up in our usual place on the terraces at Headingley the following week everyone had stories to relate about the last away trip and that was all part of the ambience of being a fan. Travelling to Fartown to play Huddersfield was always a wonderful day, the claret and gold were a fantastic side then, whose stars we feared and admired – names like Cooper, Hunter, Banks and Valentine still bring a thrill even after all those years. Parkside, to play Hunslet, saw some titanic battles over the years and of course the season used to start with a game against them for the Lazenby Cup, many of which were amongst the fiercest matches of them all. It was a tragedy that they couldn't maintain that ground because it was a wonderfully intimate, intimidating venue. By the time the 1957 Challenge Cup final came round we had a car, a second-hand Ford 10, to make the journey to Wembley – my first-ever trip to London. We went down and back in the day and it took forever but that didn't matter because of the prospect before us. Mother packed us up with goodness knows how much, there was a huge hamper of sandwiches to keep us sustained all day. Eventually we parked up in Harrow and got the tube for the first time in to Wembley Way, which made it even more thrilling and exciting.

Gordon Morrish

Wasted Journey

We struggled to Salford the other year for a Friday night Sky match but we never actually got into the ground. There had been torrential rain all day and I was hassling my dad from

Leeds F. C.
Matches arranged 1895 1896

1895	First		Second	
Sept 21	Dewsbury	Home	Dewsbury	away
28	Batley	Home	Batley	away
Oct 5	W Hartlepool	Home		
12	Hull	away	Hull	Home
19	Manningham	Home	Manningham	away
26	W Trinity	away	W Trinity	Home
Nov 2	Huddersfield	away	Huddersfield	Home
9 c *	Brighouse	away	Brighouse	Home
16 c	Hull	Home	Hull	away
23 c *	Bradford	away	Bradford	Home
30	W Trinity	Home	W Trinity	away
Dec 7	Hunslet	away	Hunslet	Home
14	Liversedge	Home	Liversedge	away
21	Batley	away	Batley	Home
21	Halifax	away	Halifax	Home
96 28	Dewsbury	away	Dewsbury	Home
Jany 1	Bradford	Home	Bradford	away
4	Brighouse	Home	Brighouse	away
11	P Church	away	P. Church	Home
18	W Hartlepool	away		
25 c	L P Church	Home	P. Church	away
Feby 1	Manningham	away	Manningham	Home
8	Huddersfield	Home	Huddersfield	away
15	Liversedge	away	Liversedge	Home
18	Wyan	Home		
Feby 22	Hunslet	Home	Hunslet	away
29	Halifax	Home	Halifax	away
Mar 7				
14				
21	Cup [x]			
28				
Ap 4				
11	XXXXXX		XXXXXX	
18	Wigan		away	

The first Northern Union fixture list is drawn up.

CLUBMATES AT LEEDS PLAYER'S HOME.

'A group taken on a visit by the Leeds Rugby League players now with the team on tour in Australia, at the home of Jeff Moores, the Leeds three-quarter. Left to right: Tom Moores, Stanley Smith, Archie Moores, Joe Thompson, Leslie Adams, and J. Lowe. An article by Joe Thompson appears on this page.

A newspaper article published during the Lions tour of Australia in June 1932.

about 4.30 to get going but he said to leave it as late as possible to allow all the idiots off the motorway and to see if the game was on. In the end we finally set off at half-past six and fought through all kinds of weather and hold-ups to get to near the Willows just before kick-off, only for GMR to announce that the match had been postponed because the pitch was waterlogged. Even the lines and markings they had painted on had been washed away. The rain had been so heavy that we lost one of the windscreen wipers on the journey because they had been on full blast all the way and it just sheared off under the weight of water. We had to stop on the hard shoulder to try and repair it but, like the game, all to no avail.

Andrew Jagger.

Surprise Stop

We decided to go to Barrow one Sunday and set off early so that we could take a leisurely trip through the Lake District on our way to the game. We set ourselves the goal of being the first Leeds fans into the town and were busy waving at all the Wallace Arnold coaches and other cars that we passed on the way over the border. We went on the old route through Penrith and after a while we seemed to be the only car on the road so we settled back to enjoy the views. As we rounded the corner of one of the big lakes we saw a lone 'Wally's trolley' parked in a lay-by. We slowed down because we were sure it couldn't be a supporters' coach as it was so far in front of the others. Then we saw a group of men jogging in single file around the shoreline. We looked at the front of the coach and it had the big team logo in the window, we had caught up the players and they were out stretching their legs and taking a breather. We pulled in and wandered over to watch and wave. Most of the guys smiled and as they climbed back on board we wished them good luck and patted them on the back. Back in the car we decided to act as unofficial escort to the team and with scarves draped out the window we led the way into Craven Park, being allowed to enter the officials car park even though we didn't have a pass. The team won a narrow victory and we prided ourselves on the long journey home that we had been a part of it.

Paul Barker

"Are You Coming Back?"

WILL HE COME BACK?

ERIC HARRIS, *whose scoring feats, and whose brilliant gifts of pace and changing-speed have made him one of the personalities of the game during the past three seasons, played his last game with Leeds to-day—under his present contract. He has declared his intention of returning to Australia shortly—but it will not be the fault of the Leeds R.L. Club if he is not induced to return.*

Twice in his three seasons he has headed the League try scorers.

His record is :—

1930-1 ... . 58 tries
1931-2 ... . 41 tries
1932-3 ... . 57 tries

This was the question the boys on Featherstone ground were asking to-day when Harris (left) and O'Rourke, the Leeds "stars," signed their autograph books. Both the Australians played their final match with Leeds under their present contract. Our picture was taken at the dressing-room door on the Featherstone ground.

Dynamic second-rower Phil Cookson demonstrates his prowess to Leigh fans.

As Luck Would Have It

When Leeds qualified for Wembley in 1994, the first time for sixteen long years, we were determined to be at the head of the queue for tickets – which was no mean feat as we were living in Worcester at the time. Tickets went on general sale after the Easter Monday game at home to Halifax so we decided to forego our holiday Sunday and set off at 4.30 on the following morning, arriving at Headingley at around eight o'clock and found ourselves third in the line. We paid for the privilege of watching the game but elected to remain in the queue so we didn't even see it. The weather was foul, there was sleet and a strong wing, but we got our coveted tickets. The irony was that before setting off, and not sure when and if we would get there or if there would be any seats left, I had bunged in a load of postal applications just in case and five tickets more arrived on the doorstep a little later. In the end I got rid of those by placing an advert in the *Yorkshire Post*.

Andy Cave

Same Venue, Same Outcome

Three times in the late forties, early fifties Leeds played in major games at the neutral venue of Odsal, Bradford and didn't win any of them. Each one became like a pilgrimage, with cars almost bumper to bumper between the two cities causing enormous congestion. For the Challenge Cup semi against

Some sample the high life: these are the early days of corporate hospitality.

Warrington in 1950, it was so bad that we had to park at the Leeds/Bradford boundary and walk miles to the ground. By the time we eventually got in there, near to half-time, the match was as good as over Warrington were so far ahead. Exactly a year later and at the same stage of the same competition, we were murdering Barrow and planning arrangements for Wembley when the Cumbrians staged an amazing fightback and we finished the match desperately trying to hold on. Arthur Clues, undeniably our hero but with a mean streak, decided to deliberately foul one of the Barrow players right out on the touchline in an effort to play out time and with the conviction that they would miss the shot at goal that would have drawn the game. When their full-back, Stretch, lined up the kick the whole ground fell silent. We were as convinced as Arthur that he couldn't possibly get it

but when the ball sailed through the posts we were crestfallen and desolate. The players must have felt the same way because they lost the replay convincingly at Fartown a few days later.

Geoff Caplan

Train Takes the Strain

Immediate post-war, the main way of travelling into Lancashire for matches was by train, which was always interesting! The carriages didn't have corridors or any form of toilet in them so once you were in that was it for the duration. Inevitably, on the longer journeys that led to some obvious discomfort. Two incidents stand out, the first was on the way to a big game at Wigan. One of our party, a member of the family who for years afterwards was

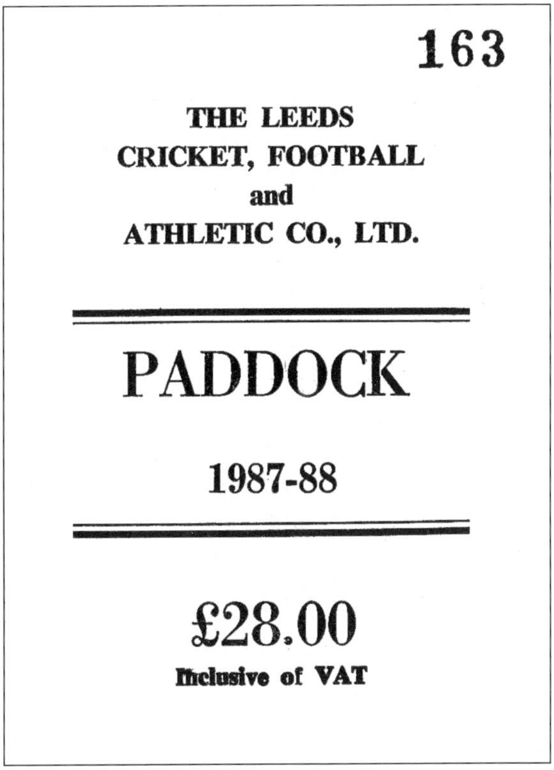

Fans have their own sacred areas; a season ticket for the Paddock before the seats were put in.

163

THE LEEDS
CRICKET, FOOTBALL
and
ATHLETIC CO., LTD.

PADDOCK

1987-88

£28.00
Inclusive of VAT

never allowed to live it down, had got into the spirit a bit too literally beforehand and was caught short midway to Central Park. As soon as he realised that we had crossed into Red Rose country he excused himself, lowered the window and let nature take its course. On the second occasion, we were heading for Cumbria – Whitehaven, I think – and were allocated a third class carriage. I was the youngest and smallest in there and because there were so many of us and space was limited, I was elected to spend the entire time tucked into the luggage rack. Apparently it was a trick borrowed from students who used to try and catch the conductors out when they travelled round Europe.

Neil Jeffries

Military Precision

This season's cup campaign nearly caught my dad unawares. He has been a fanatical season ticket holder for years and was on a fabulous six-week cruise ending up in Australia when the Rhinos beat Wigan in their opening tie. He found out the score and then realised that he would be home in time to watch the next round against St Helens – but only just. The week before we got a surprise phone call very early on the Sunday morning from halfway around the world desperate to know if we had managed to get him a ticket. He was staying with some of the old rugby clan from Headingley who had emigrated to Sydney and all talk was about the impending match. The flight was due to land at Heathrow in the early hours of

The Rugby Football League

SILK CUT CHALLENGE CUP

SEMI-FINAL

Bradford Bulls v Leeds Rhinos

at The Alfred McAlpine Stadium, Huddersfield
Sunday 28th March 1999
Kick-off 2.00 p.m.

ADMIT TO
ST. ANDREW'S CAR PARK
Via Stadium Road (see overleaf)
Follow Red Diamond Signs

J.N. TUNNICLIFFE, CHIEF EXECUTIVE

No longer Fartown, there are superb new facilities that host the big matches.

the day of the game and there was then the coach ride to Leeds ending up in the bus station at around quarter past one. Kick-off was two thirty so there was little margin for error and the arrangements had to be like a military exercise with the logistics of who had to be waiting where in case of emergencies or contingency. We had to have every avenue covered. He was on tenterhooks all the way back through the twenty-four hour flight and five hour coach journey. There was no thought of jet lag or tiredness, it was just a question of whether he would make the match. We were waiting virtually with the engine running and sandwiches and a flask at the ready to ferry him up to

Headingley. Fortunately we all got there with twenty minutes to spare and the result made the planning all worthwhile.

Sue Munden

Flights of Fancy

As you grow older and start having to do things like working for a living, it becomes harder to follow your team home and away to every game, especially if your job involves a lot of travelling around anyway. You are always checking fixture lists and schedules to make sure that wherever possible the two don't coincide. From the mid-nineties onwards the logistical problems have got worse and sometimes you have to go to quite extraordinary lengths so as not to miss your heroes. In 1994, I was travelling in the United States and managed to get a cheap flight home at short notice when Leeds got to the Challenge Cup semi-final against St Helens at Wigan. It was a hugely emotive occasion, one of the most exciting and tense ties you could ever wish to see as we battled to make Wembley for the first time for sixteen years. As soon as Ellery went in for the late try that ensured victory, my joyous celebrations were tempered by the fact that I knew I'd be delving into my savings again for the final a month later. As it turned out, that proved to be a very expensive loss! In more recent times, we were playing away at Salford one Wednesday evening and I had a meeting in Belfast that morning. I altered my arrangements by changing my flight to Manchester rather than Leeds/Bradford airport so that the trip to the Willows on my return would be easier, even though that meant making a four thirty start in the morning. Of course no-one predicted the intervening snowstorm which made the M62 virtually impassable. Despite that, I struggled to the ground, arriving at about an hour before kick-off where only about fifty other fans were waiting. The Leeds team bus got there at about the same time minus Gary Mercer who had missed it because of the weather, even though he had run three miles to the ground and he was following behind in Alf Davies' car. All I can remember is Alan Tait coming into the stand with us and

saying, 'I'm not playing out there I'll get ******* hypothermia'. Needless to say the match was called off.

Richard Stevens

CHAPTER 3

Debuts and Great Players

LEEDS

R. L. SUPPORTERS CLUB 1974-75

PRICE FIFTEEN PENCE

'A challenge which I accept' - Roy Francis

Roy Francis, the greatest coach in the club's rich history – a revolutionary who was responsible for the triumphs of the late '60s and early '70s.

A coded cablegram sent from the Leeds secretary to former player Dinny Campbell in 1927, as the search for a winger continued.

Antipodean Colossus

I had the honour of seeing Arthur Clues' first and last games for Leeds – and most of the others in between – played alongside his good friend Bert Cook. When he first ran out at Headingley, which thrilled the huge crowd, Arthur looked like a man mountain. He wasn't the biggest I'd ever seen, that was probably Frank Whitcombe at Bradford who was around at the same time and had some huge tussles with the Leeds pack, but Arthur was terrifically fast for his size. That was unusual but he also had a magnificent pair of hands and the vision of a half-back. His combination of strength, knowledge and a vicious temper made him an idol to those of us who were impressionable schoolboys at the time.

He immediately became a hero and there were many who would go to matches purely because his name was on the teamsheet. Bert Cook, who was a majestic kicker, wasn't far behind him in our affections. In those days Rugby League was much more of a kicking game between the full backs in duels to see who could out-kick who. One of my earliest memories is of Great Britain number one Jim Ledgard of Leigh punting the ball to Bert, who was a New Zealander, and back for maybe ten minutes during a game and the crowd being enraptured. Most of the Antipodeans who came over, and especially Arthur, played cricket during the summer, often for Arthur Appleyard's XI at Roundhay Park, so I got the chance to admire them all year round. These guys were always men of

The debut of Eric Harris – the club's finest ever winger is unleashed on an unsuspecting Headingley public in 1930.

the people, they were never too big not to come and have a talk to you and a bit of fun.

Neil Jeffries

Forces Rugby

Lewis Jones was in the Marines before he came to Headingley with such a fanfare and doing his national service about the same time that I was, although I was in the airforce. There were a lot of rugby league boys playing union in the forces and I played at quite a good level against some of them. Men like Billy Boston, Phil Jackson – who at

the age of nineteen or twenty was probably the finest centre in the world on his day, a phenomenal player who was so powerful – Dennis Goodwin, Brian Gabbitas and Jack Lendill, who later starred for Leeds at full back. He represented the Signals at Cattrick and they won everything for the army, even though they had virtually a side full of league players.

Gordon Morrish

David Creasser

I'll always recall the day David Creasser made his full league debut for

38

Leeds because it coincided with me getting my cat. A work colleague had a litter of kittens to give to good homes and I had just moved into my first flat and said I'd have one. I asked where he lived and he said Sandal, which was convenient as that weekend we were due to play just down the road at Wakefield Trinity. I was excited all day by both events and set off for the ground with a new cat basket. The game was marked out by Creasser's superb performance, he scored a wonderful hat-trick of tries and we won by a point. I had just enough time to celebrate before picking up my new addition, a delightful six-week old black and white moggy. We toyed with calling him Creasser but eventually settled for something more banal. Ironically he has been around longer than David, who would have been one of the all-time Leeds greats if he had not had terrible luck with shoulder injuries.

Benjamin Scott

Surprise Guest

In early 1959, Leeds signed a South African rugby union international, flying winger Wilf Rosenberg. He lived next door to my uncle out there and before he left our relatives gave him a party as a send-off because such signings were very rare at that time. My uncle then got in touch with Dad and said he had passed on our address to Wilf before he had departed. One Monday evening at about half-past eight there was a loud knock and standing there on the doorstep was the big man with greetings from Uncle Geoff. He came in and

FAREWELL GIFT

Eric Harris, the Leeds winger, who is returning to Australia, receiving a presentation from a section of Leeds supporters.

immediately we established a rapport, becoming firm friends ourselves even after he went back home.

Mel Reuben

Sad Finales

Looking back, my favourite player would have to be Andrew Ettingshausen. He had everything: grace, balance, speed, strength and drop-dead gorgeous looks! He played in some wonderful matches for Leeds and was one of those players who could turn a game on their own with a touch of magic – there were many reasons why

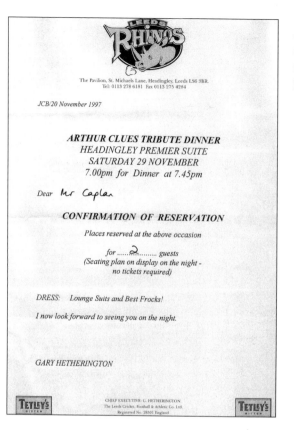

A commemoration of fifty years' association with Headingley for the Aussie icon and ambassador who never went home.

you couldn't take your eyes off him. He came over from Australia twice to play for Leeds and I can remember the excitement generated in the city when it was announced that he had signed for a second spell. That was because his first had ended in disaster and we were sure we would never see him again. Leeds had just missed out on Wembley in 1986, losing in a heartbreaking semi-final replay, and the following year, with 'ET' in the ranks we were certain that we would go one better. Wins in the earlier rounds over lesser opposition saw us draw the then mighty Widnes at Headingley in the quarter-finals and a big crowd turned up knowing that if we lost it would be Andrew's last game. That gave the occasion added tension and excitement for me as we squashed in to the South Stand to cheer ourselves hoarse. The game was really exciting although Widnes always looked the stronger and held a narrow lead late in the second half. With time running out, my man tried a chip over in a last desperate attempt to win the game. It wasn't one of his best efforts and instead of him regathering it and romping away, Widnes caught the ball and scored the winning try. We were desolate, I was speechless and Leeds were out of the cup. My despair was compounded on leaving the ground when I heard people saying how it was all Andrew's fault and he must have been paid by the opposition. Two years later, my hero returned and won a Yorkshire Cup medal. When the Challenge Cup came round after Christmas, he was in superb form again and, ironically, we drew Widnes at Headingley in the quarter finals. This time over 25,000 turned up and the atmosphere and anticipation was nearly suffocating. I was sure that the stage was set for Andrew's revenge but Widnes destroyed us by half-time and we were inconsolable for another year. The following week he finally returned home after wearing the blue and amber for the last time.

Karen Batley

The Incomparable Lewis

The greatest I ever saw has to be Lewis Jones – although I was always impressed by 'Farmer' Fairbank for some reason and the way he ran with his knees up. But Lewis was magical, there was all the furore surrounding his arrival and how great he was going to be, and he was. Still, in my minds eye, I can visualise his genius running into midfield and towards the opposition and another Leeds player coming out of nowhere and across the back of him at which point he somehow flipped the ball up behind him to his team-mate who went on a diagonal run to the line without a finger being laid on him because the defence were all still watching Lewis. They didn't see a thing – sheer brilliance.

Stuart Charmak

Worth the Damage

I'd been in the supporters' club before the testimonial match for Chris

Sanderson between Leeds and Great Britain just after Wembley in '77. I was walking up the tunnel into the South Stand just after the game had kicked off and the ball went into touch. I caught it on the bounce and threw it back to John Atkinson on the wing and immediately ripped the sleeve out of my red velvet jacket. Afterwards, in the bar, Atky said, 'that was a good pass you threw me'. I replied, 'Yeah, look what I've done here and, by the way, it was the only one you caught all night'.

Stuart Duffy

The Finest Winger Ever

I was sitting in the stand at Lang Park, Brisbane watching a game when I shouted down to my old friend Eric Harris, the legendary Leeds winger of the '30s, and asked him how it came about that he ended up as a nineteen year old from Toowoomba playing on the other side of the world at Headingley. 'It was here at this ground, which was known as Browns Field then', he told me. 'I was playing for Brisbane Wests in a game and the referee ran past me and said "Harris I hear you want to play in England". I told him I did and every time he ran alongside me he gave me little bit more information. "A man will come and see you" he said, "and you'll play for a team called Rochdale Hornets". I thought little more about it but a few weeks later a man did come to the door and my mother answered and said it was about playing in England. "Oh, so you're the agent for Rochdale" I said. "Definitely not" replied the man I recognised as Jeff Moores. "I'm the

41

Eric Harris in action.

club ten glorious seasons later: 'I had married a Leeds girl by then and we had a young son. It was early 1939 and war clouds were gathering and after a lot of soul-searching I decided that it was best to take the family home to Australia and asked for a meeting with the Chairman Sir Edwin Airey. Although small in stature – most of his players towered over him and I was six foot one – he was extremely firm. I eventually got the call to go and see him and stood, almost to attention, at the end of his desk. He looked up and asked me why I wanted to see him. "Well, Sir Edwin", I said, "I have been here for quite a while and always given of my best. I've scored 391 tries in 383 appearances – many of them vital ones, I've broken all the try scoring records for the club and always behaved honourably when representing the colours. In view of the political situation in Europe I would like to be released to return home for the good of my family and would the club be prepared to pay the passage" which was at a cost of forty-five pounds. Sir Edwin looked up and over at me and thought for a minute before replying, "There is no doubt that you have served this club with distinction. As you say, you have thrilled the crowds with some spectacular performances and won many medals. For each of those you have been very well paid, so the club will not reimburse your passage". How ironic I thought, I came for nothing and left for nothing.'

Harry Jepson

captain of Leeds and you're coming to Headingley. It's a good club, they'll pay you well if you make it and there's a new college just being built – Carnegie, you can go there to finish your studies and then they'll get you a job as a teacher". So I was on my way'. 'How much did they offer to pay you?' I asked him. 'There was no signing on fee, but after four games they gave me £450 which was a season's wages in those days'. I was absolutely amazed that he had risked everything without a guarantee, but then he told me a similar tale of when the time came to leave the

Little Maestro

One player who was an absolute delight to watch and a wonderful entertainer for Leeds was Jeff Stevenson. He was unbelievable – no one of his diminutive size should have had the kind of strength that he did. He was a beautifully balanced runner, light on his feet and so unpredictable when he had the ball in his hands. So much of the way the team played was dictated by what he did in midfield. He used to frighten defences when he ran at them and big men who used to think they were safe running at him couldn't understand why they were being driven backwards. Before him there was Dickie Williams, part of the engine room at the base of the scrum along with Ike Owens and Dai Jenkins who dictated the whole tempo of the game. Dickie was brilliant and I admired him enormously. I was very upset when he went to Parkside but an even greater sadness was when I bumped into him a couple of years before he died and he was using two sticks to walk after having both his hips and a knee replaced. I preferred to have the memory of the man as I knew him.

Maurice Gordon

Coincidence

When I decided to get involved with the Rugby League Conference, one of the first calls I had to make was to Bev Risman, who was helping to run West London. It was tremendous because Bev was one of my heroes, one of the stars who were playing for Leeds when I first went to watch them in the late '60s and he was the first name in my autograph book. When I got through to him I said, 'actually you won't remember me but last time we spoke I was five years old'. He confirmed he didn't but since then it's made me determined to find the book to prove it to him sometime. I'm sure it's somewhere in the loft at my parents' house.

Andy Cave

Lewis Jones

There was enormous interest and excitement when Lewis Jones came up from Wales and made his debut at Headingley against Keighley. I saw that match and I was at Mount Pleasant, Batley a few weeks later when John Etty broke his arm. I can still see it vividly – he picked up Lewis in a big bearhug and slammed him down on the ground. We knew it was serious when he didn't get up and Dai Prosser began demonstrating his annoyance. We all stood there, Batley fans as well, shaking our heads thinking we've spent all this money – £6,000 was a hell of a lot in those days – for a great player who we'd heard so much about and before we'd really seen what he could do he was badly injured.

Mel Reuben

A Matter of Priorities

My daughter, Louise, was born at four o'clock in the morning on 1 January 1985. I'd been at the hospital for goodness knows how long over New

One of the most skilful and gifted players ever to don the blue and amber – John Holmes in typically artistic pose.

Year's Eve and I finally decided that I had better go home and have some sleep and freshen up. My wife, who was both exhausted and exhilarated asked what time I would be back so that we could share the first day of our new-born. 'Not till after the match', I told her, 'I can see my daughter any time but Eric Grothe has arrived today and he's something really special'.

Stuart Duffy

Ahead of His Time

I guess I was spoilt by the Roy Francis era of the late '60s and early '70s when Leeds took all before them. We couldn't wait to see his teams in action because they were so entertaining. I was captivated by the new, unique style of rugby they played, for the first time it wasn't dictated by and didn't depend on forwards dominating each other early on. It was the backs that controlled the game, they were given licence to play open rugby from the kick-off and that was a revelation that made the matches enthralling. I'd watched Leeds for thirty years by then but this was an education, he refired my imagination and enthusiasm and took the game to another level which we didn't know existed. Francis revolutionised the sport and I'm not sure that it has caught up with him even now. It was how rugby league should be played, he encouraged skills and unexpected artistry amongst a group of hugely talented, predominantly local youngsters whom he brought through together. There may have been bigger or possibly better personalities in earlier years but he welded his charges into a wonderful team – probably the best ever. If any one of them epitomised

The lieutenant of Roy Francis' triumphant charges and later a cup-winning coach.

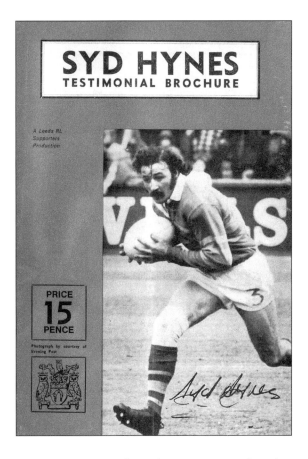

his philosophy and vision then it was John Holmes, but it was the sum of the parts that made following them so enjoyable. I bumped into Roy Francis in the Coffee Shop at Moortown a few years after he had retired and I remember begging him to come back.

Geoff Caplan

Across the City

Leeds made a big money signing in early 1961 when Brian Shaw arrived from Hunslet. It stands out in my mind because it was so unexpected. He was already an international and his signing was quite spectacular. It was secured in

secret on a Saturday morning and in the afternoon he turned out at Headingley against Leigh. The first we knew of it was when he ran out in a Leeds shirt. There was a collective intake of breath when we realised because he was so well respected and his debut coincided with a superb run of form that took us to our first ever Championship victory.

David Neale

Early Superstars

Leeds had one of their greatest teams in the 1930s and there were some superb players who joined them, but I can vividly remember the arrival of

A magnificent finisher with
destructive power on attack and
defence. Winger Alan Smith was a
player for twenty years and scored a
record four tries on his debut.

Australian Test star Vic Hey. He revolutionised back play when he had the ball in his hands, he seemed to be able to create space out of nothing. Chief beneficiary was Eric Harris – who I think we called 'The Shadow' to start with – who scored some wonderful tries. For the game as it was then, he was the best. He was so elusive the opposition just couldn't catch him, he had the most wonderful swerve and side-step and an amazing turn of speed. His vision and support play really were quite remarkable. Leeds always had first-class artists who played with great enthusiasm rather than just for money. Jim Brough was a super full-back, and a great leader, in the days of length-of-the-field kicking duels with people like Jim Sullivan of Wigan who was always an opposition player we admired and feared. Those personal battles between the full-backs were the foundations of the attacking play for the rest of the team. The best goal-kicker I ever saw was Joe Thompson, in fact I can barely remember him missing from anywhere on the field, he was very robust but athletic with it. Stan Smith was probably the fastest player we ever had although I can just about recall Harold Buck making a similar stir when he arrived. Very little in the game now is new, there was terrific understanding between Fred and Eric Harris, with their scissors moves for example, and thirty-odd years later Syd Hynes and John Atkinson were doing the same thing. There was always a great excitement when an unexpected signing was announced in the local paper, someone like scrum half Frank Watson who came from Hunslet in 1949 and made his debut against them at Parkside. There

was astonishment when we read he had crossed the city and he transformed a Leeds side, which had been at a very low ebb at the time, in partnership with the terrific Dicky Williams from Wales. Then there was Bert Cook, a quite amazing kicker for a man with a size five boot, and a lovely player alongside Arthur Clues. He was a fit, young boy when he arrived with exceptional speed and a wonderful side-step, which unfortunately caused terrible problems with his knees long after he retired. After he finished playing I got to know Arthur terribly well through business – I used to buy oil from him for my plant hire company when he was a rep for one of the big multinationals – and socially. I remember enjoying a particularly memorable flight back from Los Angeles with him after he had visited his homeland. He kept me entertained with ribald and colourful tales of his matches in Australia but he loved England and said he was never going to return home permanently. He was charming outside of the confines of the pitch, a real gentleman.

Oscar Caplan

Giants of a Generation

I first started going to Headingley when I was twelve. What fired me really was when the Australian's came over to play for us after the war. First there was Arthur Clues, then Bob McMaster and after that Ken Kearney – it was a great side. Of course, in those days, they were magical figures because we didn't know a lot about them before they arrived. You had to go and see them and they

Lance Todd trophy winners twenty-two years apart – Steve Pitchford (1977) and Leroy Rivett (1999).

were larger-than-life characters. I can remember to this day the photograph of Bob McMaster in the Evening Post with the accompanying headline, 'McMaster on the high seas'. After a while of watching them, I had to make a choice which taught me a lot. I had half-a-crown pocket money and there used to be a church dance on a Friday night that was one and ninepence which was exactly the same as it cost to get into Headingley. It wasn't a difficult decision and it turned out to be the best choice I have ever made in my life. I used to stop at home with Dad and listen to Friday Night Is Music Night and go to the

game with him on the Saturday. The next really big debut I'll never forget was Lewis Jones because we have always had a Welsh connection within the family and Great Auntie Annie wrote to my grandma just as his signature was announced to say 'Lewis is coming but don't tell anybody that he gets sick in his stomach'. Anyone with Celtic ancestry is related anyhow but we did feel that he belonged to us.

Ruth Walker

Unsung Hero

I'll always remember thinking that when Leeds won the Challenge Cup final in 1977 and Steve Pitchford won the Lance Todd Trophy for the man of the match, that it had gone to the wrong man. For me, it should have been Stan Fearnley. He stood across Wembley like a barn door and allowed Kevin Dick to play. I've always liked loose forwards, they were specialists and I think that they are lacking from the game today. If we had a little bit more craft in midfield and at the base of the scrum, I'm sure we could even beat the Aussies, but that kind of individualism has been replaced.

Ruth Walker

New Neighbours

In the early post-war years when Arthur Clues and Bert Cook came, amid much heralding of their arrival, they were put up in digs in Headingley Avenue, just opposite where I lived. They had no sooner got here than the snows came with a vengeance and my friends and I ended up out in the street

Due recognition for two of the club's finest servants.

Teenager David Creasser made a huge impression on breaking into the side in 1983.

having a huge snowball fight with them, as they were absolutely fascinated by the stuff. We didn't know a lot about them before they set foot in Leeds, but they made a massive, immediate impact and we couldn't wait to see them in action. Clues was a giant who we were grateful was on our side but full-backs like Cook were masters of their own domain in those days. The legendary kicking duels were a sheer battle of will between two opposing players, it was like chess pieces being moved about on the field of play aiming to get a crucial advantage for their team – especially as with unlimited tackles and contested scrums – possession was everything. Another who came with them who made a tremendous impression was Australian winger Len Kenny who was very small but extremely fast. He was only here for a season but he scored some terrific tries. There was one where he scorched down the sideline like a rocket only about six inches in from the touch.

Gordon Morrish

Forward Thinking

Whenever I think back to the old Leeds teams I used to so enjoy watching, I always return to the 1970/71 season and the phenomenal feats of Bob Haigh. That year he broke the world record for the number of tries scored by a forward with forty and in the intervening period much has rightly been made of the service he received from the likes of the magnificent Ray Batten and Bill Ramsey who he ran off. Haigh, though, did so much more than just pick up the pieces of their genius. Being a former scrum half in the professional game, I've always marvelled at how the forwards are so mobile around the pitch. That was Haigh's forte along with his uncanny ability to read the play and his almost extra-sensory anticipation. So much of the good work of Ray Batten would have come to nothing if Haigh hadn't been on his shoulder to take the off load. More often than not, all his tries still needed scoring and I used to love watching him hand-off opponents with huge fends or bursting through would-be-tacklers from close in to score with a combination of skill and tremendous determination. They were the kind of tries on the end of the most entertaining build-up play that kept the Headingley faithful talking for weeks afterwards.

Dave Williams

Forgotten Man

I was lucky to see Roy Francis' team grace Headingley in the sixties, who swept everything before them in the most wonderful style. What is not so well known but is confirmed by the players is that the real star behind the rise of the side was T.L. Williams, who came up to play for Leeds from Wales post-war. He was the man behind the throne, the trainer who took the players, especially the young ones, to new heights of fitness and agility, which gave Francis who was the tactician the material to work with. Williams has never really had the credit he deserves, he was always a bachelor and used to live in a flat in Cardigan Road just round the corner from the ground. He was always at Headingley, he lived and breathed for the Leeds Rugby League Club. He was always only ever known by his initials, people just referred to him as 'T.L.'. One of the finest to benefit was Mick Shoebottom, whose career was so tragically cut short. He would have broken every record in the book, he could do everything – even act like a second row forward if you wanted him to. His perception of the game was uncanny, the kind of talent that you can't coach – it's in your genes.

Gordon Morrish

CHAPTER 4

Rituals and Superstitions

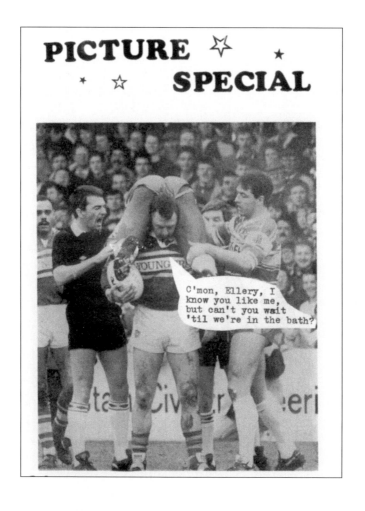

Tell-Tale Sign

Mum could always tell the result of the game from the way Dad walked down the drive after coming back from the match. If his hat was on the back of his head, Leeds had won, if it was pulled over his eyes it was going to be a very quiet tea. We got a *Green Final* every Saturday – the lad used to come down Lidgett Lane shouting and I would run out and get one – and I would let Dad read it before cutting out all the reports and pictures for my scrap book. It used to sit alongside my autograph book and the programmes, they were my prized possessions.

Ruth Walker

Banished

My whole family follows rugby league but, having been born and brought up in the South, I have to confess that it isn't my first love. I've been to a few matches, mainly at Headingley during the traditional holiday period, but more often than not the team has lost and so it has been my fault! The same is true when the rest of them watch Leeds play on the television. Whenever I am in the room they seem to be behind so I get banished to the kitchen until the final whistle so as not put the mockers on them.

Sara Steele

But Which One?

I've always had 'lucky shirts', the only problem is we kept losing in finals and semis so I had to keep changing them or buying new ones. At the last count I had four or five and I keep rotating them until we lose and then revert back to one of the others. Somehow they seem luckier when I'm watching Leeds on the telly rather than at the matches and recently I've ended up sticking to a Great Britain shirt, which seems strange.

Andy Cave

Vantage Points

One of the great rituals everybody did at Headingley was changing ends at half-time. We used to stand behind the posts Leeds were playing towards and change round at the break. More often than not the team played towards the Headingley Lane end first and we used to make our way under the cavernous North stand via the huge long tea bar and take our drink round with us. In those days, the changing rooms were at the top left-hand side of the pitch, at the bottom of the pavilion, and we used to wait for them to come back out. We always knew when they were on their way because of the strong smell of liniment that wafted over us when they opened the door to run out. We always applauded and roared them through and if we were lucky got to pat them on the back or clap them on the shoulder before we made our way up to our position. I suppose for the players of both sides it was a bit like running a

1932.

—to his third Australian tour with the England Rugby League team which he is to describe in special messages to "The Yorkshire Evening Post." Joe Thompson is also looking forward to the R.L. Cup semi-final between Leeds and Halifax a week to-morrow, as he polishes up the lucky elephants he brought back from his last tour.

Great players have their superstitions too.

Favourite replica shirts and scarves abound on the terraces.

gauntlet, especially if they'd lost, and people used to lean over the brick wall that bordered the ramp from the pitch to the sheds to shout their abuse.

Andy Cave

Home-made

When I went down to Wembley in 1957 my mother knitted me a Leeds bar scarf. It was a treasured possession and I made sure I wore it for all the major finals in the years after. When I got married it disappeared, I think my new wife must have thrown it out because it was a bit moth-eaten.

Mel Reuben

Read it in the Papers

One of the joys of being a fanatic is the constant thirst for information about Leeds. When I was older and a driver, I always used to try and time any deliveries or errands run from work to coincide with the local radio sports desks. Once when they sent me to Newcastle and I found a spot where I

Collective fervour and chanting – the rituals of sport.

could just barely pick up the signal on full volume and parked up for a quarter of an hour for fear of missing the news. I was rewarded when it was announced that Leeds had unexpectedly signed Australian winger Steve Morris. Prior to those days, the chief source of information was the evening paper and there was almost as anxious and tense a wait for it to drop through the letterbox after school as there was during some actual matches. There was the ritual unfolding of the back page and thrill of seeing if the headline was rugby or football. Lead paragraphs were read three or four times so as not to miss the slightest detail and then all the digest columns for snippets of information about 'A' team games or off-field news. Once devoured, the paper had to be

neatly folded and returned to pristine condition so that Dad thought that he was the first to get his hands on it. Unlike today, when nothing is really an exclusive anymore, then there was always the chance of opening the back page and finding a major announcement or even more gut wrenching if the billboard mentioned something about the Loiners. For no good reason I can recall picking up a *Green Un* one Saturday on the way home from a game at Headingley expecting just to read the match report of the game I had witnessed that afternoon only to find that we had signed Graham Joyce and Ian Slater from Bradford Northern. We had only been at the ground an hour or so earlier but no one had mentioned it there. When you are young and you can read reports from exotic faraway places where Great Britain were touring and eagerly scanned the details for Leeds players on the scoresheet, it fired your imagination. Or if we signed an overseas star we would want to find out all about the team they played for or the part of the world they came from before they arrived. Tea or homework couldn't start before the news had been gathered.

Steve Marshall

Elite Group

Those of us who met at 'A' team games at Headingley, predominantly on midweek nights, probably saw ourselves as the true Leeds fans – the aficionados if you like. It was as though we were a part of an exclusive club who were showing undying loyalty for the cause – especially if it was freezing cold. There was also that special atmosphere and thrill of seeing a match under lights. Sometimes the matches were dire, occasionally they threw up a major talking point or a superb piece of skill that we had witnessed as the privileged few but always the atmosphere was relaxed and knowledgeable. We knew that the players could hear our every word and, of course, we delighted in hearing them and the crunch of the tackles, but somehow there was no merit in being critical, it was all encouragement – except for the referee! He was usually someone coming up through the ranks and if he tried too hard to get noticed or hold up play we really used to let him know. In some ways it was as though we were watching a separate club. Nothing

The supporters' true voice – the rise of the fanzine, a mixture of fact, fiction and scurrilous humour.

gave us greater pleasure than seeing someone on debut or a trialist who we felt would make the grade because then we could hold court before the next first-team game and say things like, 'Watch out for…', or 'So and so's going to be great, don't forget where you heard his name first'. It was the same with opposition players, whenever we turned up for a first-team game and the other team was announced and our fans used to say 'Who's he?', we felt really important if we could tell them a little bit about the mystery man and whether he was any good or not. We always went for a drink with the team afterwards in the big bar under the pavilion, we were more like their guardians than their groupies. If they made the grade and we then saw them after a big match they

'Come and have a go if you think you're hard enough.' Steve Pitchford, David Ward and Roy Dickinson are in typical battle pose.

would often nod in recognition from those early times and we were always very proud of that shared intimacy. We also had our own South Stand heroes, players who were terrific for the 'A' team and yet never really made it at a higher level. They always seemed to turn on something really special for the select midweek crowd and we loved them for it – Norman Francis springs to mind.

Catherine Harmer

Force of Habit

Whenever I go to a game with either friends or family, I always have to go through the turnstiles last. It's like players who have their favoured position in the line or out the dressing room but I really don't know where that came from or why.

Marc Grant

Post Match

There was always a set routine after matches. We used to start off in the players' bar for a few drinks to discuss the afternoon's proceedings and then I invariably ended up taking a car full, including some of the players, down to the Smith's Arms near the parish church. It was a favourite haunt,

Wembley antics – ritual battledress makes fans feel part of the team effort.

especially for the overseas lads, which is sadly no longer there. Many happy memories were laid to rest when it was demolished. The landlord there was very tolerant and a huge fan of the side so they had licence to do virtually anything – especially monopolise the juke box. By closing time, several of the team (mainly the forwards if I remember rightly) would be standing on the tables carousing to the other customers. We then used to head up the road to The Richmond, which was more of a nightclub and open until two in the morning. The ritual at the end of the night was that whoever was remaining from the team had to get up on stage, link arms and belt out a version of Frank Sinatra's *New York, New York* whilst impersonating a can-can dancer. The sight of international prop forwards

doing that led to much hilarity and catcalling from the regulars. After that it was on for a curry, most often at Nafees in Woodhouse, where there was usually total uproar. Again the owners and waiters were very obliging, aided no doubt by a hefty bill being paid at the end of every meal. If anyone was left standing after that, the final port of call was Napoleon's Casino, principally for the bar and breakfast rather than the gaming tables. One night after an Alliance match on a Friday we varied the routine and went into town to 'TC's', where the players lined up twenty-five Southern Comforts on the bar, one for each of my years. Most of them ended up in the plants or were given away before we transferred to the Casino. I disappeared to the ladies for a little while and when I returned the lads had spent all my birthday money for me.

Jacqueline Tracey

Lucky Mascot

We've just started taking the next generation to matches with our son, Oliver, who's eight. He's been four or five times this season and he's never seen Leeds lose so at the moment he's our lucky charm. He'd watched rugby on the television but he didn't go to a live game until Boxing Day. I tried to explain to him beforehand how different it would be and that he wouldn't be able to imagine what it would be like to be a part of the crowd and to see and feel everything close up. When you are involved in an event and your team scores, it is completely different to jumping off the sofa in front of the television. He was extremely excited of course, but at the ground he never saw a score because everybody else stood up! He came with us to Wembley and it was quite an eye-opener for him. The noise and numbers amazed him at first and he was a bit quiet and after Leeds had gone 10-0 down he wanted to go home. He was really upset after all the expectation and build-up beforehand and he just didn't want to stay. We all felt like that but we told him he couldn't leave and that was all part of being a fan. As soon as Leeds scored he was jumping up and down and doing the high fives. At the end he even got bored because they were scoring a try about every two minutes. Only sport can give you that range of emotion. When I was round about his age and just starting to go to games I was chuffed to bits when I got my first scarf and my auntie knitted me a hat to go with it. At Christmas last year my parents bought Oliver the new millennium shirt and my mum found that old scarf and hat in the cupboard. She washed them and wrapped them all up for him and he was absolutely delighted and now wears them to the game, passing the tradition on. The scarf, of course, matches the new 'old' kit perfectly and it seemed fitting that Leeds wore that for the last record breaking Wembley because it is the only strip that I consider to be the real Leeds colours. It was just and right that the year they came back to the proper kit was the year that they won something again after so long.

Sue Munden

Newshound

I always kept scrapbooks from when I started to follow Leeds in the late thirties because that was the only way we ever got to read or hear about the team. In those days there was the *Evening Post* and the *Evening News* and I used to go to Stirks on Ash Road with a friend of mine, Terry Rook, who was equally as avid a supporter, and wait for the papers to come. We used to buy both, take them home, and save all the cuttings related to Leeds for our scrapbooks.

Gordon Morrish

CHAPTER 5

The Magic and Despair of the Cup

'87

There are some games that you just don't want to end. By the time we played Wigan in the John Player semi-final in late 1987, a lot of us were becoming convinced that we were never going to beat them again in a meaningful game. They were just starting their run of near invincibility and were becoming one of the most formidable sides in history. We had struggled to get this far, Whitehaven should have beaten us in the first round and we suffered an excruciating win over at Springfield Borough – the worst team left in the competition – in the quarters. Talk between us all before the game with Wigan was of damage limitation, we were worried that, being a televised tie, we would get shown up in front of the nation. A few minutes into the game and Lee Crooks left the field with a dislocated shoulder and that was it for us. The Wigan fans were jeering and then got right into us when they scored. I can't remember what it was that turned the game around but some things I'll never forget: Peter Tunks playing the game of his life in the Leeds pack (it was the only time he really looked like an Australian Test player whilst at Leeds) a miraculous try-saving, flying tackle by Marty Gurr on Henderson Gill when all seemed lost, Garry Schofield's magical solo try from nothing (I can still see Steve Hampson's face as he was completely wrong-footed by the sweetest of side-steps) and Schoey's swallow dive between the posts and broad grin. Finally there was the piece de resistance with the game already virtually won – Steve Morris' impudent lobbed pass to send Colin

Maskill over virtually on full-time to really rub it in. We had never imagined that we were capable of beating Wigan so comprehensively and 19-6 in a semi was a thrashing. I had never been to Burnden Park, Bolton before that day and I think I must have been the last person out of the ground. We just sat there in the empty stand, right in line with where Schofield had dumped Hampson, and savoured the feeling of reaching a final despite being underdogs and having won right on Wigan's own doorstep. There is nothing quite like it in sport and recalling it still makes me smile.

Garry Morrell

'82

I don't think I'll ever forgive Widnes. They were never really a team I hated, especially after we beat them at Wembley in '77, but memories of the cup semi-final at Swinton in 1982 will haunt me forever. We played so well that day, even though referee Fred Lindop seemed to be giving everything to the Chemics – and with a pack as hard as theirs they didn't need a second invitation. I stood facing the twenty-five yard line at the bottom end and as I'd hoped it was the one we were attacking in the second half. When Kevin Dick fed Dave Heron off the back of a scrum and he squeezed between Gregory and Myler to put us 5-0 up we started singing 'Wemberlee, Wemberlee' like we really believed it. But Tony Myler always worried me. If he had remained fit throughout his career he would have been one of the

Victory celebrations in 1932. The team pose with the spoils after beating Swinton in the Challenge Cup final at Wigan.

very best and he always seemed to save up his finest displays for us. He put John Basnett over for a try and then the same player scored another in the identical spot – on the side where we didn't have a proper winger! They led 6-5 and we were seriously panicking about our proposed trip to London. I vividly remember feeling physically sick as the clock ticked down. I was screaming myself hoarse when we had the ball but I couldn't even speak when they were in possession. When Les Dyl scored, again just in front of us, with about eight minutes left we went wild. He grinned as he put the ball down and we just hugged anyone and everyone we could get our arms round. The last few minutes were torture as we were camped on our own line and they seemed to have about five clear-cut chances to win. We kept scrambling them away and all I could bear to do was look at

my watch. Just before the final play I said 'that's it we've done it' but I'd reckoned without the cruellest kind of fate. Mick Adams' 'Hail Mary' kick as the whistle was about to go looked more like a gesture of hope than anything else. It seemed like it was going to go dead but then everything appeared to go into slow motion. Somehow the ball bounced off the crossbar and standing beneath it not even looking was Widnes centre Keiron O'Loughlin. I don't even think that he meant to catch it but it landed in his arms and he literally fell over the line to win the game. We were stunned, devastated and rooted to the spot as the Widnes fans who hadn't already made their way to the exits went mad. I remember trooping out the ground in astonished and complete silence. I couldn't stop grinning and shaking my head – it must have been delirium I suppose, but my sister, who

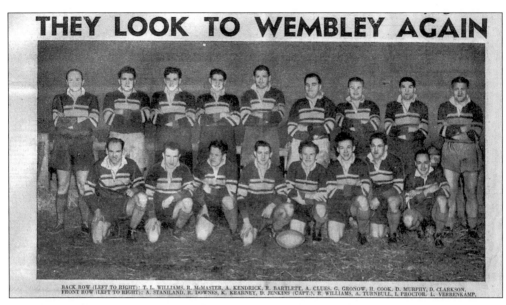

THEY LOOK TO WEMBLEY AGAIN

BACK ROW (LEFT TO RIGHT): T. L. WILLIAMS, R. McMASTER, A. KENDRICK, R. BARTLETT, A. CLUES, G. GRONOW, H. COOK, D. MURPHY, D. CLARKSON.
FRONT ROW (LEFT TO RIGHT): A. STANILAND, R. DOWNES, K. KEARNEY, D. JENKINS (CAPT.), R. WILLIAMS, A. TURNBULL, I. PROCTOR, L. VERRENKAMP.

The Leeds team that lost to Huddersfield in the cup quarter-final included 'superstars' Arthur Clues and Bert Cook.

was in her twenties, was sobbing and repeating 'It's not fair' and my uncle had tears in his eyes as well, especially as he had come up from London for the game. I hated Widnes after that, and especially O'Loughlin who I'd never rated. To make it worse they gave us some fearful beatings after that in the following years: in the John Player Final when we were lucky to get nil, in a humiliating Challenge Cup semi, and once in the League at Headingley when they nilled us again and seemed to be taking the mickey towards the end. They say that a semi-final is the toughest place to be a loser and after Swinton '82 I can vouch for that. I honestly don't know how the Leeds lads who played that day could ever bear to put their boots on again.

Paul Barker

'68

Everybody can remember the watersplash Wembley in 1968, it is one of those occasions that is always replayed – with Eddie Waring's famous commentary. Unfortunately I wasn't allowed to go as I was only seven at the time and my dad thought that being part of a crowd of 100,000 would be too much and too dangerous. I'd already been to a few matches at Headingley by then and in the week before the match collected all the posters and clippings to put on my wall. As compensation for not being there I was given a cap, scarf and rosette and packed off to my cousins to watch the game on television. The end was incredibly tense and I couldn't bear to watch it, diving behind the back of the sofa as Don Fox lined up the simple conversion that should have won the cup for Wakefield. I couldn't really take it in when Eddie shouted 'He's missed it, he's missed it.' We were dancing and leaping around the room, waving our scarves and singing – it was almost as good as being there. In the end I forgave my dad when he brought me back a programme which had pride of place on my wall for years afterwards.

Phil Smithson

'78

RUGBY LEAGUE CHALLENGE CUP SEMI-FINAL
Odsal Stadium Bradford
1st April 1978 3·00pm
FEATHERSTONE ROVERS V. LEEDS

BIG
Match
Official Programme 20p

The Challenge Cup semi-final of 1978 coincided with my seventeenth birthday so it was a memorable day all round. I was having an all-night party at my mum and dad's in the evening – the first time I was allowed to do something so decadent – and I'd invited friends from all round the country, many of whom came up that afternoon to take in the match against Featherstone. None of them had ever been to a game live before and the excitement was made even more acute by me being their guide and commentator. We travelled to Odsal in a convoy jammed into four or five cars and even my description beforehand that Odsal was a unique bowl built on an old rubbish tip didn't prepare them for the culture shock they were about to experience. We were a gang of about seventeen strong and soon mingled in with the South Standers around the halfway line. They asked for interpreters and subtitles as we sang awaiting our favourites and having told them to cheer for the blue and ambers, we turned out in our change strip of white! I was pleased, though, because I always thought that we looked bigger in white. By the time the match started any

explanation of the intricacies of offside were unnecessary as it was all-action stuff. At half-time we moved out of the crush and nearer towards the try line that Leeds were attacking. We were in the perfect place to see my hero John Holmes dummy and go over to score what was effectively the winning try. On the final whistle we rushed up the bank to slap our heroes on the back as in those days the players had to climb the hill to the dressing rooms at the top. I think it took them about three-quarters of an hour before the sea of fans parted to let them through. It was probably more exhausting than the game for some of them! We left the ground singing about Wembley and the lads with us from places like Luton and Brighton were saying how much better an atmosphere it was than football where the fans were segregated. Just then, as we passed a line of Wallace Arnold coaches lining Odsal Top, a group of Featherstone fans wearing Manchester United scarves rushed past and pushed us into the side of the waiting buses leaving me to look sheepish and apologise all round – fortunately memories of a fantastic match took precedence over what became a very long night.

Steve Marshall

'71

Coming back from Wembley in 1971 we must have set a record for the fastest journey to Leeds. My dad had just bought a new car, a white Toyota sports convertible, and there were five of us squashed into it – including three generations of our family. We couldn't wait to get away from the ground after the ignominy of the defeat against Leigh. We were such huge favourites

Y.E. News, Monday, May 13, 1957. Tel. Leeds 27241—28041.   5

They brought back the cup

The Rugby League Challenge Cup is back at Headingley after 15 years. Keith McLellan, the Leeds skipper, is chaired by team-mates as he holds aloft the Cup at Wembley.

Don Robinson, who scored one of the vital tries, goes over the line for the third Leeds score. Jeff Stevenson, who won the Lance Todd Trophy (best individual display), dances with elation.

Burly second-row forward Don Robinson, held by three Barrow men, ploughs on relentlessly while referee Mr. C. F. Appleton watches on.

A near miss for Leeds as Keith McLellan is pulled down just short of the line during a Leeds onslaught.

An historic day: Leeds win the Championship for the first time in their history amid wild emotional scenes at Odsal. The date on the programme was a misprint – it was 1961!

THE NORTHERN RUGBY FOOTBALL LEAGUE

CHAMPIONSHIP FINAL

LEEDS
v
WARRINGTON

at
SATURDAY
20th MAY - 1960

Odsal Stadium
BRADFORD

Kick-off 3.0 p.m.

OFFICIAL PROGRAMME   Price 1s.

that we couldn't lose but we did and embarrassingly. Once we had found the car and weaved through the London traffic up to the motorway, Dad just took off. I'm sure that he was hitting well over 100mph at certain stages and we were back home in under two hours. Throughout the entire white knuckle ride, no one could bring themselves to say a word. We just sat there squashed in and dumbfounded staring out the window in disbelief in total silence like we'd been to a funeral. We didn't even put the radio on for fear of hearing a match report. It's amazing really, I can't remember anything about the game but the journey back is still vivid.

Howard Brooks

'84

It might not have had the glamour of some cup finals, but for me the John Player success in 1984 was one of my most memorable days supporting Leeds. There was drama – on the field and off it when we lost half the family – snow and food, for me the perfect combination! We had a feeling that we might win, but the weather in the week leading up to the match had been pretty abysmal and we thought that might favour their bigger pack, especially as we relied on the artistry of our backs like John Holmes, David Creasser and Dean Bell. The weather and a fairly sizeable contingent from Leeds made slow going to Central Park because of debris on the

M62 after a night of howling gales. Parking round the ground there has always been notoriously difficult and everyone was trying to get as near as possible as kick-off time approached without success. Usually we got a space behind the Working Men's club opposite the ground but we were forced further towards the town into a road we hardly knew. Because we could hear the roar as we locked up and grabbed our flasks, we took little notice of our bearings, the younger ones amongst us running for the turnstiles at full pelt. We caught our first glimpse of the pitch just as Widnes scored their first try right in front of us with the opening attack. We had intended to get shelter but because we were late we ended up standing on the open terrace behind the posts, one of which had snapped from the winds of the previous night. It was an unfamiliar position but we soon found a knot of Leeds fans and began singing just as the boys started to hit back with some wonderful rugby to take the lead. The second half was a brutal affair as the forwards literally slugged it out at times. Mark Laurie was like a giant that day mowing down the beefier Widnes forwards with copybook tackling which was a trademark of the Australian game and an eye-opener for British fans. As the game wore on and Leeds resolutely attacked the end we were at our jeering of the Widnes players for their over-zealous tactics got louder and more intense. Just before the end, with Leeds holding on, their prop Steve O'Neill was sin-binned and we vented all our pent up spleen on him as he ran down the tunnel next to us. The fact that the Loiners had won in the face of extreme intimidation made the victory so much sweeter. We cheered the lap of honour and walked slowly back to the car as the sky clouded over, dissecting the match. Unfortunately, because of the rush to get in, a couple of our party had lost their bearings completely and we stood around for nearly an hour frantically looking for them. Eventually they appeared on the horizon in completely the wrong direction having left the ground by the wrong entrance and we set off. It was virtually dark and deserted as we wended our way through Westhoughton and when the snow began to fall it was thick and settled immediately. By the time we joined the motorway, the outside lane was covered and impassable. I have always loved the snow and in defiance of its worst we stuck our scarves out of the window and ploughed on towards Leeds as it became nearly impassable over the top of the Pennines. Getting through was almost as nerve-wracking as watching the game. When we finally made it into the centre of Leeds, the city was almost deserted because of the weather but we decided we had to mark the occasion of Leeds winning a trophy. We were famished by now and decided that we would treat ourselves to the best meal we could afford. We ended up at the Skanda in the Merrion Centre that boasted the biggest mixed grill in town. We did it justice washed down with a few beers and then set off down Merrion Street for a massive snowball fight. The perfect end to a memorable day.

David Townsend

'94

The Challenge Cup semi-final win in 1994 against St Helens at Central Park must rank as the greatest game I've witnessed. We seemed to be defending all afternoon, protecting a slender lead, before the greatest player I've ever seen, Ellery Hanley, crossed for two spectacular late tries. I can recall a pal of mine screaming, 'It's E, it's E' as he loomed up in support for the first one that effectively won the game and the pitch invasion that followed the final whistle. The feeling of going to Wembley for the first time for my generation was unbelievable, the closest I've been to crying, and I was just as high as a kite as we left the stadium. It was absolutely brilliant.

Andrew Jagger

'94

It was a hot day at Wembley in 1994 especially if, like me, you were wearing a replica Leeds shirt. What with the emotion and sickening excitement of the occasion – it was the first time I had been to the Cup Final, even though I had followed the team for years – and the after-effects of a glass of wine at a pub near Kings Cross at lunchtime, I was feeling pretty faint. When Schoey scored in the corner in the second half, just near where we were sitting, and it looked like we might win, I honestly thought I was going to keel over. I could feel myself going and it was only that all the Leeds fans were swaying on their feet that I managed to remain upright. After a few deep breaths I gradually

THE RUGBY FOOTBALL LEAGUE
THE WILLS 1969 EUROPEAN CLUB CHAMPIONSHIP

LEEDS
(ENGLISH CHAMPIONS)

PERPIGNAN
(FRENCH CHAMPIONS)

at
Headingley, Leeds
SATURDAY, 15th NOVEMBER, 1969
Kick-off 3.15 p.m.
Official Programme   1/-

Leeds won the inaugural European Club Championship, a great idea that failed to become an annual event as anticipated.

began to come round but unfortunately so did Wigan. By the end of the match I had regained my balance but Leeds had lost the cup.

Lynn Belvedere

'68

We didn't go to many away games, but made an exception for the Challenge Cup semi-final against Wigan at Swinton in '68. We absolutely took them apart and I remember coming away from the ground with a huge grin and my father saying, 'that should have been the final, it was a truly great game'. Of course we then went to what became the Watersplash Final and witnessed aquaplaning rather than rugby, which all came down to Don Fox's last-gasp kick by the posts to win it for Wakefield. Neither my brother or father could watch, they both had their heads in their hands hiding their eyes, so it was left to me to do the Eddie Waring bit – 'He's missed it, he's missed it!' I seem to recall that we collected the trophy and paraded it on our lap of honour with Trinity's ribbons still on it because the dignitaries didn't have time to change them again. They'd already swapped them over several times during the dramatic last few minutes.

Stuart Charmak

'72

One game I will never forget, a real major event, was when Leeds beat St Helens in the Championship Final in 1972 at Swinton. My schoolteacher

DEWSBURY	
(Red, Amber and Black)	
1 Adrian RUSHTON	Full Back
2 Greg ASHCROFT	Right Wing
3 Alan CHILDE	Right Centre
4 Terry DAY	Left Centre
5 Jeff YOWARD	Left Wing
6 Allan AGAR	Stand-off Half
7 Alan BATES (captain)	Scrum Half
8 Graham BELL	Prop Forward
9 Mick STEPHENSON	Hooker
10 Trevor LOWE	Front Row Forward
11 Jeff GRAYSHON	Second Row
12 John BATES	Second Row
13 Steve HANKIN	Loose Forward
14 Steve LEE	Substitute Back
15 Harry BEVERLEY	Substitute Forward

Referee : **M. J. NAUGHTON** (Widnes)

LEEDS	
(Blue and Amber)	
1 John HOLMES	Full Back
2 Alan SMITH	Right Wing
3 Syd HYNES	Right Centre
4 Les DYL	Left Centre
5 John ATKINSON	Left Wing
6 Alan HARDISTY (captain)	Stand-off Half
7 Keith HEPWORTH	Scrum Half
8 Terry CLAWSON	Prop Forward
9 David WARD	Hooker
10 Bill RAMSEY/Tony FISHER	Front Row Forward
11 Phil COOKSON	Second Row
12 Graham ECCLES	Second Row
13 Ray BATTEN	Loose Forward
14 John LANGLEY	Substitute Back
15	Substitute Forward

Touch Judges : **E. GRANTHAM, J. A. HARKER** (Hull)

The teams for the 1972 Yorkshire Cup Final at Odsal, which was won by Leeds 36-9. Dewsbury got their revenge at the end of the campaign when they took the spoils in the Championship decider.

who was there was a big mate of Alan Hardisty's and he got us into the changing room straight afterwards. It was magical, the trophy was on a table near the door and all the players were singing and celebrating and ruffling my hair as I stood there in disbelief – tremendous. Then I noticed, sitting in the corner of the dressing room watching everything, Mick Shoebottom, one of my idols, whose career had been so tragically ended a year before when he had been needlessly injured playing Salford. It made the memory even more poignant.

Andy Cave

'57

I was fifteen when Leeds began their run to Wembley and I can vividly remember every round. We met Wigan at Headingley first up in an historic game. The crowd was huge and before the kick-off the fencing went down at the Kirkstall Lane end. In those days they didn't have a wall, it was merely a wooden barrier, and there was such a crush that it just gave way. Officially there were over 38,000 in but we always reckoned that there were at least 45,000, maybe more, which would have been a ground record. We sat on the straw across on the other side by the South Stand and we were leaping about so much and playing around that I lost all my money. Billy Boston scored two great tries for Wigan just in front of us and it was just like watching a runaway express train. In the next round we got Warrington up here and the game was played in an absolute

blizzard. The second-teamers were stationed on the pitch sweeping the snow off the lines to keep the match going because the referee could have abandoned it. There were 22,000 sandwiched into the ground and there wasn't a soul behind either goal except for one idiot who looked like the abominable snowman by the time it finished. Both the South and the North stands were heaving and the atmosphere was tremendous. For the quarter-final, my father took me to Halifax and Thrum Hall was full to bursting after being made all-ticket. After about five or six minutes we were ten points down and we all thought 'That's it' but Leeds fought back for a memorable win. After the game I ran down to the changing rooms to collect autographs as usual and heard all the players singing this tune called 'Keep Right on to the End of the Road'. I told my father and he mentioned it to someone he worked with called Snowden, who wrote for the *Rugby Leaguer*, who printed the details in the paper and from then on it became known as the club song. We were huge favourites in the semi-final against Whitehaven at Odsal. None of us had ever seen them play because in those days you didn't see a lot of teams from across the Pennines because the majority of fixtures were regionalised and there were separate Yorkshire and Lancashire league tables and championships. The pitch was thick with mud that afternoon and for twenty minutes in the second half they just held onto the ball, taking drive after drive as it was unlimited tackles. It was so frustrating to watch and we just couldn't see how Leeds were ever

Memories of a sensational comeback in one of the best Cup Finals witnessed at Wembley.

Bamford gets the best out of Leeds

Leeds 18, Widnes 10

By RAYMOND FLETCHER

MAURICE BAMFORD has achieved in just two months as coach of Leeds what he had failed to do since turning professional 30 years ago.

The defeat of Widnes in the John Player Special Trophy final at Wigan on Saturday was the first time he had been involved with a trophy-winning side as player or coach.

Yet he spent the first hour of his moment of glory shrugging off the congratulations to heap praise on his players. "They are the ones who have done it," he said. "Coaches don't win matches."

Bamford is too modest. Ten of the players who did so magnificently on Saturday were also in the side that was humiliated 58-2 by Queensland shortly before Bamford took over.

Since his arrival Leeds have remained unbeaten in nine matches and conceded only three more tries than the 11 they let in against Queensland.

The players' tribute to Bamford is in the way they have responded to the first half and though his call for more pride, dedication and commitment.

It was all there on Saturday as they fought back after being 6-0 down in the second minute to score two brilliant tries and come out on top in a second half battle of attrition.

Discipline was not the least of Leeds's assets. While Widnes became as wild as the weather Leeds refused to be intimidated and did not concede one penalty for a foul.

Widnes conceded seven and had Steve O'Neill despatched to the sin bin two minutes from the end.

The contrast in attitude was summed up in the clash of scrum-halves. Dick was mischievous but in control for Leeds; Gregory was niggling and quick tempered.

If Gregory remains favourite to tour Australia

this summer, Dick must now come back into the reckoning. His best effort on Saturday was in supporting a sweeping Leeds movement to reach back and take Keith Rayne's pass one-handed and lunge over near the posts. Dick also threw out the long pass that sent away Leeds for their first try, scored by Holmes. But the key figure in the build-up to both tries was Laurie,

who proved to be a man for all seasons.

Last September he helped Parramatta win the Grand Final in Sydney and on Saturday he was the outstanding player at freezing, wind-blown Wigan.

Laurie gave a typical Australian second row display of hard running on attack and swift covering in defence.

He was clearly the most progressive forward in the elements eventually cloaked the teams in anonymity Laurie stood out with a late breakaway that confirmed his winning the man of the match award by an overwhelming Press vote.

Another important factor in the Leeds victory was Creasser's goalkicking. The young centre landed five out of six in a swirling wind, including two when faced with only half a target — one goal post having been snapped the day before.

Many thought Burke's kick after Widnes's second try had curled inside the imaginary post but the video recording justified the touch judges' no-goal decision.

Burke succeeded with just one of his three kicks at goal but was responsible for giving Widnes a flying start when he charged on to Gregory's

pass in great style and then turned the ball inside for Linton to touch down in the second minute.

It was an indication of the challenge Wilkinson faced in the duel of two hefty and powerful full-backs. Although the Leeds No. 1 did not achieve anything as spectacular he produced another rock-like performance and after Burke misfielded a high kick late on Wilkinson could feel he had at least held his own against Britain's full-back.

If Wilkinson's display was a nudge to the tour selectors, Keith Rayne's was a shoulder charge delivered with the same impact that rocked Widnes time and again.

The Leeds No. 8 is now arguably the most effective prop in Britain.

But it was essentially the pack's work as a unit that laid the foundations for Leeds's victory.

Ward was a brave and inspiring leader, reluctant to leave the battle even after damaging a rib late in the game. He was still in pain when he went up to lift the trophy.

"Nothing was going to stop me from doing that," said Ward who was a playing substitute on the other occasion Leeds won the trophy back in 1973.

The only other survivor from that final was Holmes, a full-back then and a hard-working stand-off on Saturday.

Hughes, Elwell and Adams were making a record sixth John Player final appearance for Widnes with the last named returning after a long injury lay off to emerge as one of their few successes.

It was from Adams's perfectly-placed kick that Lydon leapt to score Widnes's second try and remind Leeds of the kicking magic that robbed them of a Wembley place in 1981. But they were not to be outdone this time.

No stopping Kevin Dick as he charges in for the second of Leeds's tries on Saturday.

Trophy final facts

HOW THE SCORING WENT: 2 min.: Linton (Widnes) try, Burke goal 0- 6
9 min.: Creasser (Leeds) penalty goal 2- 6
12 min.: Holmes (Leeds) try, Creasser goal 8- 6
22 min.: Dick (Leeds) try, Creasser goal 14- 6
30 min.: Lydon (Widnes) try 14-10
Half time 14-10
57 min.: Creasser (Leeds) penalty goal 16-10
74 min.: Creasser (Leeds) penalty goal 18-10
Scrums: First half — W W W W L L 2-4.
Second half — W W L L W L W 3-3.
Penalties: First half — W L W L L W 3-3.
Second half — L L L L L W W W W L L L 9-4.
Hand overs — Leeds 2.
Sin bin: S. O'Neill (Widnes) 78th min.
Man of the match: Laurie (Leeds).
Attendance: 9,536.
Leeds: Wilkinson; Prendiville, Creasser, Bell, Andrew Smith; Holmes, Dick; Keith Rayne, Ward (Capt) (Squire 72 min.), Kevin Rayne, Moorby, Laurie, Webb. Non-playing substitute: Hague.
Widnes: Burke; Wright, O'Loughlin, Lydon, Linton; Hughes (Capt.), Gregory; S. O'Neill, Elwell, Tamati, Gorley, Whitfield, Adams. Non-playing substitutes: J. Myler, Prescott.
Referee: Mr. W. H. Thompson (Huddersfield).

Change in attitude

DAVID WARD, the Leeds captain said their had been a big change in attitude among the players since they suffered several heavy defeats in the early part of the season.

"We had a bit of soul searching to do," admitted Ward. "We got together, talked it out and things started to go right.

"Maurice Bamford's arrival as coach made a difference in that he took us back to basics."

Maurice Bamford congratulates man-of-the-match award winner Mark Laurie

West Yorkshire League — Hemsworth 12, Fairburn 2; Goldthorpe 12, Upton A 2.

Leeds defy the elements and the Chemics to take the John Player Trophy in 1984.

going to get possession. All of a sudden they lost the ball and Jeff Stevenson dropped a goal from a long way out and that was it, we were at Wembley. A lot of people said that he had punted the ball, but we were too delirious to care and going mental behind the posts despite being saturated. I couldn't really afford to go to the final because I was still at school but my uncle who lived in South Africa sent me some money and we went on a Wallace Arnold bus, leaving at midnight. We travelled down the A1 and it took about six-and-a-half hours to get to London but then they just dropped us off outside the stadium a full eight hours before the kick-off. We were starving and at a loss what to do so we got the tube into the centre of the city which was an experience. After the game we went to celebrate at the pub on the end of Empire Way because the coach back wasn't leaving Kings Cross until midnight. All the adults were getting drunk inside and we were having a marvellous time singing and dancing in the car park. Then we went into the centre of London and it was amazing because everywhere you looked you saw the blue and amber all over the place. There were even some fans dancing in the fountains at Trafalgar Square – it was marvellous. We got back in time to greet the team outside the Town Hall on the Sunday. All the players were on the balcony singing 'Keep right on…' and I felt wonderful, especially because I had broken the news of it being their theme tune to the general public!

Mel Reuben

'88

When I was nine I went to the 1988 Yorkshire Cup final and was completely bored by the proceedings. My dad was Lord Mayor at the time and he was presented to the teams and my cousin Chris was the Castleford mascot. I sat in the directors' box reading a book the whole time except for looking up when Schoey and Gibbo scored their long range interception tries for Leeds. I didn't become a fanatic until a couple of years afterwards but I regret not taking more of an interest in that game, especially when I went to school on the Monday and everyone was talking about what a great match it had been and how privileged I was to have seen it from such a good vantage point.

Steve Killgallon

'47

We went on a family outing to Wembley by train the day before the final and stayed overnight at the Waldorf Hotel. I can remember walking into this huge foyer, the like of which I'd never seen before, with a rattle and running round the lounge spinning it for all I was worth – which led to an almighty telling off. The morning of the match we went to Regent's Park Zoo, which was another eye-opener, and then took the tube to the Empire Stadium. The sight was amazing and overpowering and that sensation has lived with me longer than the details of the game which we lost causing me to cry my eyes out. A couple of weeks later we played

Two spectacular interceptions bring the Yorkshire Cup back to Headingley in 1988.

Bradford again, this time at Headingley, when the official record attendance was set. The old ground was overflowing and the pain of Wembley was soon forgotten.

Geoff Caplan

Heartbreak

It was so crowded near the dug outs at Swinton for the 1982 Challenge Cup semi-final against Widnes that I ended up sitting on the top of it because it was the only way I could see. Leeds were within one play of going to Wembley – which would have been my first – and we were all getting ready to run on to the pitch and celebrate. I was in the process of congratulating Ian Wilkinson who had come off with quarter of an hour or so left when Mick Adams put up his fateful kick that bounced off the crossbar and into the hands of a team-mate who scored. I don't know who cried more,

Owen Lewis Jones proudly holds the Challenge Cup and a picture of his exceptional grandad hoisting Keith McLellan in 1957.

me or him but both of us were inconsolable.

Tracey Collins

'57

Everybody has a cup run that is indelibly stamped on them and mine is the year Leeds won the Challenge Cup in 1957. In the first round, against Wigan at Headingley, I still have a vivid picture of the Wigan stand-off Dave Bolton fly-kicking the ball standing opposite the middle of the South Stand and his leg went – I can still see that now. In the semi-final against Whitehaven we were transfixed as Leeds finally got the ball and came virtually the length of the field so that Jeff Stevenson could drop the winning goal that took us to Wembley and I'm still not sure to this day if he punted it through the posts. I tried to wear the same clothes throughout the cup run and that became something of a ritual which we still do now and have a laugh about. We travelled to Wembley by car, picking my brother up who was in the RAF at the time in Buckinghamshire, and went on from there. I'll always remember coming out after the game and seeing Jimmy Dunn, the Leeds full back who hadn't made the side for the final, on one of the walkways crying his eyes out – he really was. I used to teach swimming at the time at Blenheim School and, although

Rhinos fans celebrate the moment they realized that the Challenge Cup was about to have blue and amber ribbons attached to it after twenty-one long years.

he was just a bit before me, Delmos Hodgkinson who scored at Wembley on the wing for Leeds used to be in that team so there was an added affinity. We came straight home afterwards, like I've always done and I prefer. We went just to watch the rugby.

Ruth Walker

'71

I still don't like talking about Wembley in 1971. We were sitting near the tunnel as Alex Murphy was stretchered off after Syd Hynes had supposedly flattened him and he looked like he was to all intents and purposes dead. As he passed us he most definitely turned and winked at the crowd before jumping off and returning to the field, where he orchestrated Leigh's win. I have hated him ever since that moment. Sport is all about having icons you adore and characters you despise and he is still top of my list, even though it was nearly thirty years ago.

Sue Munden

'79

Leeds got the Premiership final in 1979 – partly due to the fact that they avoided a fixture backlog during the terrible winter because of their

Super League's first Grand Final – the atmosphere was sensational, the result just less so.

undersoil heating, but then Headingley has always been at the forefront of innovation, and faced arch rivals Bradford at Fartown, Huddersfield. We'd been eliminated in the first round of virtually all of the other competitions but had gone for years winning at least one trophy a season. This was the last game of the season and the final opportunity to keep the run going so we were all desperate to go and cheer them home. Dad managed to get tickets from a friend in Bradford and we found ourselves right in the middle of some extremely vociferous Northern fans who made up the bulk of the crowd and whose numbers were swelled by some Bradford City fans as the football season had just finished. In those days football was beset by hooliganism and violence and I had to admit that for the first time ever at a rugby occasion I felt in fear and intimidated – it even got to the stage that I dare not even cheer when

Leeds scored. In fact, the Loiners were superb and completely dominated the game for one of their most comprehensive-ever victories. Unfortunately, I didn't feel like I could join in. It was one time when we won a cup that I couldn't wait to go home.

Richard Stevens

CHAPTER 6

Headingley is Home

Paul Sterling scores one of the most memorable tries ever seen at Headingley against Adelaide.

SELECTION COMMITTEE held _Pavilion._ _Sepr 18ᵗʰ 95._

Present _Maulon. Watts. Hudson. pickles. Smith. Moyes & Knaggs_

LEEDS   _v._   _Brighouse_

To be played at   _Meadingley._   Date   _Sepr 21. 1895._

First.   TEAM

		TEAM SELECTED	TEAM PLAYED
1	Back	D. Walker.	S. Walker
2	Three-quarter right	M. Mainstock	H. Haindock
3	Three-quarter centre	R. Walton	R. Walton
4	Three-quarter centre	M. A. Close.	Wright
5	Three-quarter left	J. Clarkson	Clarkson
6	Half back right	J. Barlow	Barlow
7	Half back left	J. Midgley	Midgley
8	Forward	J. Pickles. Cap.	Pickles Capt
9	,,	J. Riley	Riley
10	,,	R. Gregg	Gregg
11	,,	M. Parfitt	Parfitt
12	,,	R. Armstrong	Armstrong
13	,,	M. Fletcher.	Fletcher
14	,,	O. Hills	Hills
15	,,	D. B. Else	Oliphant
Reserves		B. C. Oliphant.	
,,			
Touch Line Judge			
Touch Line Judge			
Referee			

The first side to represent Leeds at home in the new Northern Union in 1895.

The Deciding Test

I had been to loads of Leeds matches at Headingley when the old ground had been pretty full, but it was nothing like the atmosphere for the deciding Test of the 1978 series between Great Britain and Australia. Looking back, I still can't believe that the official attendance was given as just under 30,000. The ground officially held 33,000 then and an hour before kick-off we were jammed in solid and just couldn't move. I looked round at this sea of faces everywhere and the old place was packed at every point. We ended up jammed in near the floodlight on the corner of the South Stand and the Eastern Terrace. It wasn't our favoured position but it was as near as we could get to where we wanted to be and it was directly in line with the tryline – so we were in the perfect position to see all the early Australian tries that effectively won the series! The atmosphere was sensational especially because there were no away fans, obviously, and we were all screaming ourselves delirious as the sides came out. The Boulevard and Wilderspool are known for their hostility towards visiting teams but I would have been intimidated if I had been an Australian player that day – not that they let it show. There was such a mixture of people there too, almost every club shirt must have been represented, and we were wedged between Hull and Hull KR fans who had obviously travelled together despite their differences which had been put aside for the day. We were used to changing ends or nipping out for a drink at half-time but it was impossible that afternoon, in fact I can remember feeling horrified when one of

One of the biggest crowds of the modern era witnessed the Ashes decider in 1978.

the big lads from Humberside shouted 'mind yer back' and proceeded to wee into a large Coke bottle during the break.

David Townsend

Unbeatable

I suppose I was spoilt really, growing up in the Roy Francis era. I can't so much remember exact matches or scores, but it seemed like going to Headingley meant seeing carnival rugby from Leeds every other week. Those were the days that we were the real entertainers with a team renowned for throwing the ball about and scoring spectacular tries. We weren't bothered if

A programme from the 1957/58 season commemorating the first visit of Blackpool Borough to Headingley.

A highlight of the calendar when the tourists come to call.

OFFICIAL

6d.

PROGRAMME

LEEDS
Rugby League Football Club

RUGBY LEAGUE FOOTBALL

LEEDS

v.

AUSTRALIA

FRIDAY, 24th NOV., 1967

Kick-off 7.30 p.m.

the opposition scored three tries, we just knew that we would get at least four. We weren't arrogant – although towards the end of his reign we were starting to expect to win things – but we always used to try and guess on the way into the famous old ground how many we would win by. Everyone knew that we wouldn't win many away games, especially in Lancashire where we had an awful record at some clubs. That might have been because we reserved our champagne rugby for Headingley.

Garry Morrell

The Most Gallant of Losers

As far as I know Leeds only ever played Bridgend once, in the Challenge Cup preliminary round in the depths of winter 1985. It was a game neither side really wanted, Leeds because it was an extra match in an already crowded schedule and the Welshmen because they were struggling and were liable to get flogged. Added to that it snowed really heavily, making their journey a nightmare and the pitch at Headingley virtually unplayable. The match should have kicked off at three and we struggled to get there an hour or so before kick-off, even though we lived just down the road from the ground. We were told that the game would definitely be on and that Bridgend had set off, but as kick-off time approached and passed, the majority of the crowd who remained resorted to having an almighty snow ball fight on the cricket ground which was superb. Their coach finally arrived about twenty past four to a massive cheer, with the Leeds fans running alongside and applauding the Welshman off the bus and clapping them on the back. They had got changed on the way in and declared themselves ready to play, despite a seven-hour journey, which drew more massive cheers. Several in the Leeds ranks were Aussies who had never seen, let alone played in, snow, among them Eric Grothe. Within minutes of the kick-off he had scored a hat-trick of tries and was totally unstoppable, his big bushy beard coming up covered in snow as he dived in for one of his trademark scores in the corner. He eventually went off with suspected hypothermia and, after Leeds had ensured a massive victory, they deliberately stepped off the gas to save the gallant Welshmen further unfair punishment. When the visitors scored the sole try, the three-and-a-half thousand fans who so appreciated their efforts raised the roof, especially as it was rumoured that their coach driver had been named as a reserve because they had been unable to pick up enough players on their way through because of the weather.

Phil Smithson

Fire and History

There are two vivid recollections from Headingley in the 1930s, the fire of 1932 and the only game ever played on the cricket pitch in 1938. I was there that Easter that the old North Stand caught fire whilst we were playing Halifax, standing behind the posts. It was both frightening and exciting to see the way it was demolished so quickly. There was no panic, everything was very orderly and calm and there was a kind of reverential quiet as the structure gradually became more gutted. The Christmas Eve game against Salford on the cricket ground was thrilling and fascinating. The rugby pitch was frozen I think and the decision was made to play it on the other side. The crowd packed round the perimeter and we were all out in the open, there was no cover against the elements, but because there were so many hemmed in together there was a warmth against the chill.

Anthony Camm

Our Religion

Just opposite the Skyrack pub near the ground, where we always meet up before a game, there is a church. Standing on the pavement outside sipping a pint I have often witnessed disagreements between the vicar and those going to the match, desperately trying to find parking spaces, who have tended to block his entrances which he has tried to keep free for Sunday worshippers. Once, he was patrolling

The revelry begins in the famous South Stand.

his gates in full regalia when an old Escort pulled up and about eight lads fell out of it dressed in their scarves and shirts. The driver, who had parked almost diagonally to the pavement was just about to lock the door when the verger shouted across, 'You can't park there like that, this is a place of worship'. Quick as a flash, one of the gang replied, 'No, that's where we're off and we're on a mission from God'.

Benjamin Scott

Through the Ages

Going to Headingley was always the highlight of the week, especially when we were coming across from the east of the city. In the early years I used to travel on the back of my dad's scooter which always made it a bit different. I'd sit on the wall behind the posts and Dad would stand up on the terraces behind me. As I got older, and started to grow up, I always used to try and get into the South Stand for the second half. It wasn't just that you didn't have to pay by then but was because my mate was always in there with his twin sister and she was absolutely gorgeous. Dad still stood where he always did but by then I always used to wander off – usually in search of Susan Lavis. It was a bit like a right of passage. My mum used to go when she was a kid and her great memory was the smell of cigars filling the air during the traditional Boxing Day morning fixture. All these working-class people who had got their

85

cherished cigar for Christmas and met to smoke it together at the game which gave that match, quite literally, a unique atmosphere.

Andy Cave

Perfect View

Leeds were playing Widnes in 1990 and a fight broke out amongst all the players right in front of us. We were egging them on as the referee lost control and started flapping his hands, leaving the police to run on and separate the sides. In the end there were a couple of

sin-binnings as things calmed down but you don't seem to get real square-ups like that any more. Those kinds of confrontation are great, especially if you are a twelve-year-old. Nor do you mind huge scores if your team wins. That same season Leeds murdered Barrow 90-0 at Headingley and my hero Hugh Waddell scored what was probably his only ever try for the club in that game. I was standing in the paddock with my brother waving an inflatable plastic bat and calling out his name as he walked back and was preparing to line up for the kick-off and he looked over smiled and acknowledged me, which was a great moment. His try was worth all the rest of

The history and tradition of the dual Test arena means as much to Australians – the name of Headingley is famous throughout the world.

them put together. We always stood in the same place, just to the left of the dugout, because we liked to hear the coaches shouting their instructions and the players calling to each other. You could see and feel the tackles in close-up and grimace with them but that was before all the seats were put in and a lot of the magic was lost.

Steve Killgallon

Like Nowhere on Earth

In the early days I used to come with my dad and sit on the wall. Headingley always felt huge. In the early sixties, when I was ten or eleven, I used to sometimes come over even when there was no match on and the ground was always open. I used to stand on the terraces and look around and think how wonderful it was. Occasionally, I used to make my way on to the pitch and pretend that I'd run round all the St Helens or Wigan team of the day or scorch up the South Stand side to score a length of the field try – it is a magic place, wonderful. I never wanted to do anything other than stand behind the posts at the pavilion end.

Stuart Duffy

Grandeur

The thing that always struck me about Headingley, even as a youngster, was that it was by far the smartest ground. I used to pride myself on the fact that I had visited every other one and at most of them it meant standing on bricks.

Even places like Central Park and Fartown, that had terrific history and atmosphere, when they were full didn't have the quality of Headingley – it was the Rolls Royce of venues. Because we spent all summer across the other side watching Test, county or local league cricket, it became both literally and metaphorically our second home.

Neil Jeffries

To Any Lengths

I've always had this emotional bond and attachment to the team and the atmosphere at Headingley. There are no lengths I won't go to in order to support them. I don't have much money but it doesn't matter, you do whatever you have to when following your team – it's something only a fanatic would understand. Twice I've flown back from Australia to see Leeds in the Grand Final and then the Challenge Cup. People ask me why, but after listening to the Bradford semi-final on the internet at four o'clock in the morning, there was no decision. I was at the travel agents four hours later to book the trip back, whatever it cost. Until 1 May 1999 it had been nineteen years of heartache, an entire lifetime, waiting for them to win something which is why I was in an indescribable paradise floating around Wembley after we had beaten London, topped up by the homecoming at Headingley the day after – you live for those precious moments. I started watching from the main stand but about the age of fifteen transferred my allegiance to the South Stand. Now I go to Melbourne Storm every other week

LEEDS R.L.F.C.

BASS HEADINGLEY

SUPPLIED BY ROCK PROMOTIONS - 0744 451414
Ingredients: Sugar, Glucose, Permitted Colours and Flavours

One of many commercial enterprises, an attempt to sponsor the stadium never really caught the public imagination.

but it's not Headingley. No matter how far away I am, this is my spiritual home and I hope it never changes. Of course it needs re-developing but I hope the atmosphere and mystique never leaves.

Marc Grant

Final Place

I've always stood at Headingley. I started off in the Boys' Enclosure, which was at the left-hand side of the South Stand and then I graduated to behind the posts with my friend Elaine. There's an indescribable magic about the whole of the stadium. I can walk through the gates irrespective of whether the ground is empty or there are few standing around watching an Academy game and I am home and it always has been like that. When I go I

want my ashes spread across the South Stand side.

Ruth Walker

Value for Money

Going to Headingley is like having one big extended family, you just feel comfortable in the intimate surroundings. Leeds traditionally do well at home and you go there knowing that you are probably going to enjoy the game, which helps. The best Leeds sides have always played entertaining rugby whether they have won or lost. I remember once when we were teenagers, I dragged one of my friends, Amanda, along and we sat on the wall waiting for the game to finish. We ran on at the end in an attempt to pat our heroes on the back and all I could think

A famous face in the crowd.

was 'God, they stink!' – it was the embrocation but it remains a vivid sensual association with the ground.

Sue Munden

Greatest Kicks

I'm not actually a devotee of Leeds Rugby, more Leeds United, but I've been to a lot of the major matches, mainly in the cups. My record's pretty good: I seem to be able to pick the ones they win and some of my friends who are fanatics often ring me beforehand just to check that I am going! Headingley, though, holds memories as a playground in the summer. We often used to wander down there, the gates always seemed open, and throw a ball about on the pitch pretending to score spectacular tries. I used to try my hand at goal-kicking and once I managed a successful conversion from nearly on the halfway line in my outdoor shoes. It was just for a laugh, we were betting how far we could kick the ball and I just jokingly put it on the centre spot and sent a friend round behind the posts to act as touch-judge. He couldn't believe it when the ball sailed over his head. One of my friendships nearly ended over kicking a ball around on the famous turf. We only had the one between us, an old over-inflated brown leather one that was coming apart at the seams. I put in a huge kick for touch and the ball sailed over the TV gantry and onto the South Stand roof. We stood around for a while waiting for it to roll back down but of course with it being 'U' shaped we never saw it again – for all I know it's probably still up there. We decided against climbing the spiral staircase and had to just head off home instead arguing about whose fault it was and who was going to pay for a replacement. The other 'game' we used to play when cars were parked on the rugby pitch if the cricket was on – which we always thought was sacrilege – was to check all the names of the season ticket holders painted on the backs of the seats in the main stand just to see if we could recognise friends, family or celebrities. If you got to that level you were either posh, rich or normally both.

Howard Burleigh

During the War

My earliest recollection is more of Headingley rather than rugby. I would have been about seven when war broke out in 1939 and I can vividly recall the troops coming back from Dunkirk all bloodied and in a very poor state walking down Kirkstall Lane. We lived virtually opposite the ground and my mother and father, along with all the neighbours, ran out to take them in. Within hours of that happening the ground was opened up as a rehabilitation centre. The tea huts were used for the soldiers to be billeted in to allow them to recover and re-establish themselves, or as a base after they had been discharged from the various local hospitals. It was my first

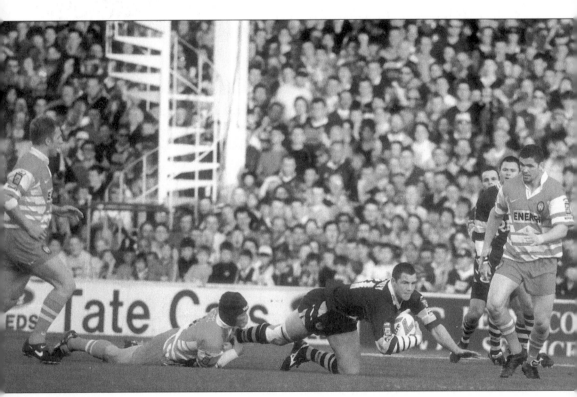

The spiral staircase in the South Stand: an endearing landmark but a nightmare for commentators taking their position.

The ethos of Super League: a full house on a glorious summer evening.

serious impression of the stadium, even though I had been in there watching with my father from the age of four, and it remains a lasting and unforgettable one. Living so close, it was like having a palace on your doorstep and we were in there all the time, winter and summer, watching or playing one sport or another. As well as the rugby and cricket, I've seen top class athletics and cycling up there and one of the biggest events used to be the annual Printers' Sports Day. For rugby matches we always went behind the goals at the Kirkstall Lane end – we had a mortgage on our own spot – and I used to stand there with my father until he died when I eventually got a seat in the stand. We knew so many people there and we'd all meet at the first league match and shake hands and wish each

other a good season. It was a very close atmosphere and I've found that with rugby supporters in general wherever I have gone or we have met up for a chat. Whenever I'm there it always feels very, very comfortable – a real sense of belonging – it's been a part of my life for all of my life. Just walking through the gates brings memories flooding back. Mention Leeds abroad and people might not know it but as soon as you say Headingley, Leeds then you're on the same wavelength – it must be a marketing man's dream.

Gordon Morrish

Right Image

To the best of my knowledge, Leeds have never re-signed a player once they have let him go and very few, if any, have ever asked for a transfer out of the place. That's part of the aura of Headingley it means as much to the players as it does to the fans once they've sampled it at its best. There's also many examples throughout the eras of great players who have suddenly left or been surprisingly transferred because their behaviour or reputation wasn't deemed as appropriate, particularly if there was any chance of the club's good name being tainted. No matter who has worn the famous colours no-one is bigger than the club. I think it was Douggie Laughton who commented when he left that he hadn't realised how big the Leeds job was or what he was taking on until he got there. At Widnes, if he wanted anything in the papers he had to call them up. When he started at Leeds he couldn't understand why his phone rang at eight o'clock every morning with press men asking him if there was any news or if there was any truth in the constant rumours regarding likely signings.

Brian Davies

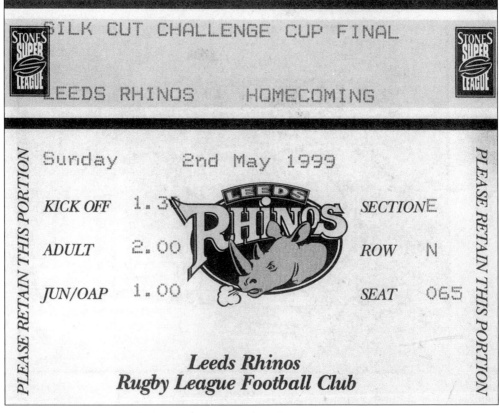

Winning the cup was special – bringing it home was equally so.

CHAPTER 7

Away Days

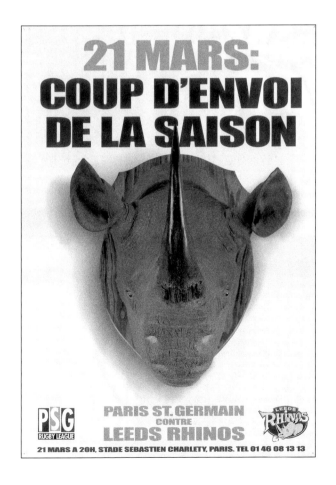

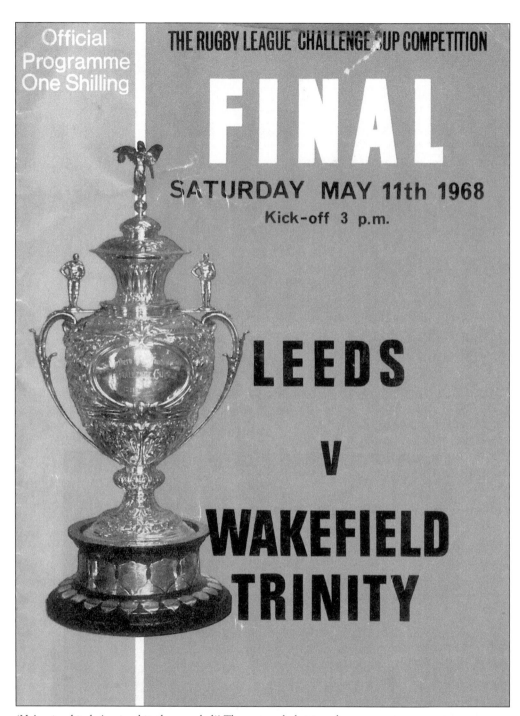

'He's missed it, he's missed it, the poor lad!' The watersplash triumph.

'Oh We Don't Like to be Beside the Seaside'

When we drew Blackpool Borough away in the first round of the John Player in 1983 we thought it was superb. An excuse for a great weekend away and then a chance to give the no-hopers a thrashing on the way home. The first part of the plan went rather well, we arrived on Saturday lunchtime and headed along the front to find a set of digs. The first one was rejected when one of the girls objected to nylon sheets but round the corner we found a nice homely landlady who seemed genuinely pleased to put us up. Lunch was the obligatory fish and chips and then we hit the usual piers, prom and pleasure beach. The night is something of a blur, I know we did some kind of pub crawl but strenuously avoided going into 'The Manchester'. We had some difficulty finding our temporary residence in the dark but eventually crawled in and were resuscitated by a traditional breakfast. Pre-match entertainment was a trip up the Tower from where we picked out the ground and once we had arrived it became obvious that it looked better from up there. The eighty minutes of action proved to be probably the most excruciating of my Leeds rugby watching. No-one outside the real fanatics had turned up because the result was a foregone conclusion and I think the players must have thought that as well. It was one of those occasions when early in the second half I honestly felt like running on and playing myself because I couldn't possibly have done any worse. We were behind virtually all the way through and we were thinking of seeking asylum in the Isle of Man rather than face going home when John Holmes pulled out a piece of magic in injury time for us to scrape a totally undeserved win. As we filed out the ground in virtual silence we shook the hands of every Blackpool fan and apologised to them. I don't think I've ever been so embarrassed leaving a game – you know how to deal with defeat when you've followed Leeds through the years but this was a victory that was hard to swallow. Of course from there we went on and won the competition, playing some great rugby along the way and the memory of how we got to the final was instantly forgotten, but this was one time that the match spoilt what was otherwise a superb away trip.

Simon Close

Gatwick

I guess it must have been sometime in the early seventies, my mum and dad booked us on a package holiday to Spain. It was exciting because it was our first trip abroad as a family – I must have been about ten or so – but it was over Christmas and it meant missing the traditional Boxing Day fixture against Wakefield at Headingley, which I was none too pleased about. The journey to Gatwick was an absolute nightmare, there were huge snow drifts and it took us nearly three hours just to do the last few miles into the airport. Having struggled to get there we found that there was a twenty-four hour delay to all flights and we were snowed in. Nearly everyone was distraught or complaining but I was delighted because it meant

John Holmes strides in for the first of Leeds' tries in the 1984 John Player final. The journey to and from Central Park for the match was fraught, but worth it.

that I could watch the game on the television because it was traditionally an 11.30 kick-off and featured live on Grandstand complete with Eddie Waring's unique commentary. We were packed into the small TV room in the departures lounge with everyone mystified or disinterested in what was going on and me leaping about at the front cheering on the team like a lunatic and shouting at anyone who wanted to turn over. I'm sure we won and we eventually did get to take-off so it worked out okay but it was probably the strangest way to watch a 'home' game.

Phil Smithson

Featherstone

Around the time I was starting to go to away games regularly we went to Post Office Road, a ground where we didn't have a particularly good record. It was completely different to the space at Headingley, a real cramped community stadium packed with hostility and atmosphere although there were lots of Leeds fans there because we were playing well at the time. All through the morning there had been heavy fog and we were convinced that the match would be off, especially as when we got there we could only see half the pitch from where we were standing. The teams ran out with Leeds playing in

An Australian pin-badge commemorates the World Club Challenge – a great idea but an inevitable outcome.

their white away strip but that didn't help. The referee decided that he could see both try-lines from the middle so the match kicked off but we could only see the end that Featherstone were attacking and judge what was happening by our defensive line moving backwards and forwards and the cheers or jeers from across the other side. We could hear the kicks and the occasional grunts in the tackle and sometimes cheered a player running back to collect the ball. Midway through the first half there was a stifled groan and the Tannoy announced 'Tryscorer for Leeds, David Ward' and we all leapt up and down as if we had some idea of what was going on. Soon afterwards the match was abandoned with Leeds still ahead and we all booed that we had been denied a famous win that we couldn't see. Later we found out that Neil Hague had actually scored the try and we lost the re-arranged game.

Steve Marshall

Old Trafford

I'm not exactly a youngster and I have been to Wembley to see Leeds and to most of the big games but when the team emerged with Wigan from the tunnel for the first-ever Grand Final at Old Trafford in 1998 I couldn't stop crying. Just looking at the Leeds end and seeing that shimmering sea of blue and amber just got to me. It's something about those unique colours, when you

HULL F.C.

Welcome you to the Boulevard

25p

Slalom Lager

RUGBY LEAGUE

CHAMPIONSHIP

H U L L

v

L E E D S

SUNDAY, 19th OCTOBER, 1980

Today's Match is Sponsored by

GLENROSE (Fish Merchants) LTD.

see them together it can only mean
Leeds Rugby League. The eventual
outcome was really disappointing but
nothing will compare with that
overwhelming tide of emotion I felt
before a ball was even kicked. It will
live with me forever.

Lynn Belvedere

A Rude Awakening

I made a real mistake the first time I
went to the Boulevard in Hull. I had
heard how fierce the crowd were there

but I was only about nine and I was
determined that I was going to proudly
wear my Leeds scarf. We parked the car
the other side of the railway bridge near
the ground and my mum and dad and I
began the walk round. We got a few
disparaging looks and some less than
complimentary comments but I wasn't
that bothered because I was there to
support my team. My mum, in
particular, was becoming increasingly
anxious and asked me to put my scarf
under my coat at least until we made it
through the turnstiles but I refused. Just
as we were waiting to cross the road a
group of Hull fans in their late teens

98

came up and surrounded me and started pointing and poking at the scarf saying that they wanted it. When I refused – and at this stage my mum was really starting to panic – they threatened to burn it, with me in it! I must have looked like a startled rabbit in headlights and they just howled with laughter and walked away. It taught me a lesson about 'territory' and I have to say that although I've been back a few times to the Boulevard I have rarely had the courage to wear a prominent scarf.

Garry Morrell

Barrow

I'll never forget going to a cup-tie at Barrow. We sat at the top of the ramshackle stand and when you looked out over the back you could see right into the men's toilet because it didn't have a roof on. At half-time, as it was a freezing afternoon there was a huge cloud of steam that hung over the men as they stood facing the brick wall and if the wind blew in the wrong direction it felt and smelt like you were enveloped by a cloud of acid rain.

Andrea Tracey

By Any Means

My first away game would have been to Huddersfield in the late twenties. We went to Fartown on a coach run by some private company – there was not the supporters' club there is today – and it was a tremendously exciting experience for a youngster, a chance to join and meet new, unusual people who all had rugby in common. We discussed the game endlessly, learning all different kinds of perspectives and analysis of players and tactics which we had never heard of or considered. The other match that really meant something was against Wakefield and we used to beg for lifts to Belle Vue if there was anyone in the neighbourhood who had access to a car. After the war we travelled to Cumbria for matches by train, which used to take over six hours. We were packed up with sandwiches and orange juice or lemonade and it was a full-scale excursion that took the whole weekend. The journey back was overnight and invariably the trains were late or slow and stopped numerous times at every tiny town or village but it gave us time to fully discuss the game we had seen, reminisce and look forward to the next few fixtures and plan the details of the following proposed trip to somewhere like Wigan or Swinton. It was like a pilgrimage, watching rugby league and boxing was such a large part of our lives. Going to Hull, it was the ladies' section of the crowd who used the most appalling language. We were always the 'Jew' team and whenever one of our players used to make a good run they would scream 'Get back to Jerusalem'. There was never any trouble though, if anything got a bit out of hand someone would voice their disapproval or issue a threat and that would be it – crowds in those days were self-policing.

Oscar Caplan

The Twin Towers

The most emotional I have ever been about rugby was walking out of Wembley tube station and seeing those twin towers at the end of Wembley Way in 1994. I had been told by friends who had been there before just how special it was to take that walk, especially when your team is playing, but I couldn't begin to describe the feeling. We had been there on coaches, in 1990 to see Great Britain, which had taken us right to the door but it didn't have that same sense of magic of actually walking past all the vendors in a swaying crowd singing your heart out. The best thing to do is make a full day of it, to have the build-up in Leeds on the Friday night arguing about all the possibilities for the following day, travelling down early in convoy with all the scarves and banners on the cars and coaches, mingling with all the fans at the services and then travelling back on the Saturday night to share the craic in town. A couple of times we've stayed over in London and made a weekend of it, but it's a lonely place to stay – especially if you've lost.

Andrew Jagger

Wakefield

I went to Belle Vue with my dad when I was about twelve. He is a God-fearing man, in the choir and a regular churchgoer, but we were getting some real stick throughout the early stages of the game. I had a replica shirt on with number two Jim Fallon on the back and some Trinity fans began spitting on it from behind. The next thing I knew my dad had turned round and smacked one of them in the mouth. It was totally out of character and a complete surprise but we weren't bothered again.

Dave Armstrong

Another World

Once you become part of the rugby league family you just don't want to miss a game. I was once in Hull visiting some friends who supported the Airlie Birds and they were playing St Helens at the Boulevard and asked me to go with them. I readily agreed but they told me it would mean going into the notorious Threepenny Stand. As Leeds were not involved it was hardly like taking my life in my hands and I thought it might be an interesting experience as long as no-one heard my accent. Their renditions of 'Old Faithful' were amazing and made me shiver so goodness knows what effect it must have on opposing players. Any of them who came near the stand side suffered volleys of abuse, much of it extremely witty it has to be said – although some of the words were completely beyond my comprehension. When it got to near half-time there was movement at the back of the cramped area and I suddenly realised how big the Hull fans were compared to the ones I knew at Leeds. The whole of the stand seemed to have emptied when just four men standing right at the back went stomping off in search of refreshment. It was then that I understood why they kept chanting 'We all agree dockers are harder than miners'.

Paul Barker

Leeds provided the opposition for Halifax's last first-team match at Thrum Hall.

A Right Hammering

I don't think I've ever been so desolate at a game than I was at Leigh for the final league fixture of the 1982/83 season. We hadn't played particularly well that year and were entering a fallow period after fourteen unbroken years of trophy-winning and we travelled to Hilton Park without any real expectations. The contrasts between the two teams and their respective grounds couldn't have been more stark and I remember when we arrived getting some fearful verbal abuse from three or four old ladies leaning over the rail round the pitch drinking tea from huge flasks. The game was awful, we were totally inept and the mocking and baiting by the home fans just got progressively worse. I was praying for the match to end and to be put out of my misery from just after half-time, especially as my hero John Holmes was playing and I didn't want my vision of his genius tarnished. By the end we had experienced total humiliation, especially as Leigh scored with virtually the last play of the game to register a half-century of points against us. I'll never forget the score, it was 51-2 and it felt like it was brandished on my forehead as we slunk away amongst the howls of derision. That was the first time that I had experienced my beloved team conceding such a landmark and there is still a little bit of hurt tucked away in me somewhere even after all this time.

Howard Brooks

Little Boy Lost

One memory that will never leave me is getting lost on the way out of Wembley in 1971 after Leeds had been humiliated by Leigh. I was only about eleven at the time and we had parked on the edge of London and got the tube in to the stadium. Somehow, in the midst of the huge crowd that meandered up Wembley Way and into the underground station I managed to lose my dad. We were jammed in and suddenly he was gone and I have this vivid picture of standing at the top of the stairs looking down to where you could hear the trains and feeling absolutely terrified. I couldn't see him anywhere and I obviously looked lost because some British Transport staff took me into some dingy office and started to ask who I was. By now I was totally petrified and unable to speak but after a few minutes my dad came in and found me. After that, the pain of defeat didn't seem so hard to bear as the feeling of relief was overwhelming.

Andy Cave

After the War

One of the first away games I went to was at Salford. My father took me on the steam train and we got off at Seedly station and walked through the back streets, where a lot of the houses had been bombed during the war and they hadn't started rebuilding them yet. We got to the ground and stood on the terracing behind the posts watching the great Arthur Clues play. That same year we went to Castleford,

again by train, and then caught a bus from the station to Wheldon Road. In those days there was no cover there, just the main stand and that was it. It was a diabolical snowy day but we braved the elements to see Leeds win again. I was so badly affected by the cold that day that we came out of the ground about a quarter-of-an-hour early and I tried to get warm on a single-decker bus back to Leeds that went all over the place before it arrived home.

Mel Reuben

Wigan

The virtual Championship decider in the 1989/90 season was on a Thursday night when Leeds, who were second, had to go to Central Park to face the league leaders, Wigan. It was an enormous game which was narrowly lost but left two abiding impressions. One was John Bentley throwing his opposite number Mark Preston into the advertising hoardings, which we thought was fantastic, and the other was my dad, who was normally so reserved, screaming 'Whitfield you're a crook' over and over again at the referee. We didn't get back until after midnight because we had to stop on the journey home at Birch services for my best mate to throw-up. He was exhausted and emotionally drained because it was the latest we had ever been allowed to stay up for an away game and it turned out to be a fitting epitaph.

Steve Killgallon

Wembley '57

I went to Wembley on the Leeds and Hunslet schools trip with my name tag on and a packed lunch of an apple and a banana. Before the match the coach went to the Tower of London, which would have been excitement enough for a boy who had never been out of Leeds. There was almost a hint of disappointment when we had to get back on the coach but we soon remembered why we were there. I can't recall anything much about the game, more how we waited in line outside to have our names ticked off and then trooped through as a group into the imposing ground, bigger even than we had imagined, to take up our places. We were handed the sheet of words for the community singing and belted out some of the songs. When Leeds had won, they made a point about coming over to our section of the ground to show us the silverware and we shouted until our throats were sore for our heroes. Not surprisingly, the journey back was almost silent as none of us had an energy left and nearly everyone slept virtually all the way back.

Ken Fawcett

Disowned

I was sitting in the main stand at Thrum Hall on a typically miserable, freezing cold day with my dad surrounded by die-hard Halifax fans. Leeds were underperforming, which was not a surprise, but I was getting increasingly frustrated and taking it out on the referee and the home players – I think the word 'cheat' may have been used on a number of occasions – and I was getting louder and less ladylike as the match progressed. Eventually two old men behind us tapped Father on the shoulder and said, 'Excuse me but is she with you?', at which point he turned round and said 'Absolutely not' and that he had never seen me before in his life.

Jacqueline Tracey

Paris

We never thought that we would go to such an exotic location for a game or travel to a match by plane – it certainly beat Castleford on a wet Wednesday! The first year Leeds played there, in '96, it coincided with my father-in-law's sixtieth birthday and we flew him out there as a surprise. He turned up at Stanstead airport with no idea where he was going and we ambushed him at the departure lounge with the match tickets for all of us. Being a huge Leeds fan he was as delighted as he was surprised. When we arrived we went to a little bar and sat there having a drink trying to work out how to get to the ground whilst studying an entirely inadequate map of the suburbs of Paris. We plucked up our best Franglais and tried to ask a waiter directions to Charlety to which he replied in perfect English, 'Yeah, just get that number 43 bus there' which happened to stop right outside and went direct to the stadium. We probably looked a bit odd in all our Leeds regalia, especially amongst the locals returning home from work but

Charlety Stadium, Paris – a short-lived but enjoyable venture for players and fans alike.

the roles were reversed when we took our seats and were surrounded by passionate French fans setting off flares and waving flags. It was really exciting and quite surreal to think that we had gone on an expedition just to get to a game. You had to pinch yourself that you were there.

Michael Collins

Kells

When you're a fan there is no logic to what you'll do. One year Leeds got drawn against Cumbrian amateurs Kells in the preliminary round of the Challenge Cup. It was a match that nobody wanted and one we were never going to lose and was scheduled for a Wednesday night at Whitehaven. We decided on the spur of the moment to go up there on a supporters' bus – it may even have been the only one that went to the game – for no other reason than it was the start of the cup trail and if Leeds went all the way we could say that we had been there throughout. It was a long, tortuous journey followed by a particularly lousy match during which Kells probably wouldn't have scored

Fulham's finest hour as the fledgling club put the giants of the game out of the cup.

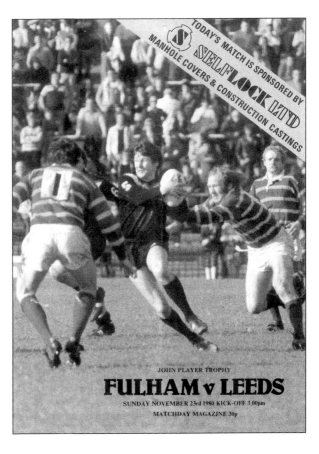

even if the Loiners had walked off, and we played like we really didn't want to be there. The only thing I can remember is pulling down the slope into the Recreation Ground at twilight and seeing Sellafield glowing in the night sky through the rain to welcome us. We should never have gone, we couldn't wait to get out and it took forever to get home but we'd do it all again if the need arose because we are mad.

David Townsend

Fulham

We received a double shock at Fulham soon after the Londoners had come into the league. We drew them in the John Player and got beaten despite being huge favourites. We were a massive scalp for them. Things went from bad to worse as my uncle, who had moved down to the capital from Leeds, offered to drop us back at Kings Cross for the train journey home. He took it as an opportunity to show us how the natives drove and bragged about his newly acquired skills: mounting pavements, cutting up taxis, shooting down bus lanes, cornering without signalling – it was the most unwelcome of white-knuckle rides and nearly as bad as the one we had already suffered at Craven Cottage.

Lisa Parke

Envy

Wherever we have been, it doesn't matter which ground you go on, there has always been jealousy of Leeds. That's why everybody wants to beat us and they always have done. We were at Featherstone the other year when Doug Laughton was the coach and I bumped into him just outside the dressing rooms and he said, 'I had no idea what the Leeds fans went through when they went away' – obviously they had been at him. You've got to stand your corner when you support Leeds. That's one of the reasons we so cherish the sanctuary of Headingley.

Ruth Walker

Fartown

Soon after I started following Leeds we went to a game against Huddersfield when they were still playing at Fartown. Though a famous venue, it had obviously seen better days and as we stood up on the really steep banking I was struck by the long grass and moss growing through it. I could image the ground full when Huddersfield were a fantastic team and it seething with people craning from on high to see their heroes in action. It felt quite eerie, like the ghosts of famous players from the past were all around. A bit like Headingley, you could actually live the history and tradition of the place.

Jim Munden

Disaster in the Capital

When Leeds got back to Wembley after sixteen long years in 1994, we were determined to get the best possible seats and make a full celebratory weekend of it. We settled for two £40 tickets as near as possible to the Royal Box in case the boys actually won so that we could be in prime position to see them raise the silverware. We made arrangements to stay over at some friends who lived near Edgware so that we could take in the full atmosphere. I had put the tickets in my handbag for safe-keeping when we left Leeds on the Friday afternoon for the drive down. Next day we were raring to go and as we were preparing to leave to catch the tube my husband said to me that it was likely to be hot and crowded and it would be better to leave things like my handbag safe back at the house, which I did with no thought that our prized possessions were still in there. When we got to the ground the realisation dawned on me that I had left them behind and a furious row ensued, me blaming him for interfering with my routine and him going spare that I had done something so stupid. For about an hour we pleaded with the stewards on the gate and those in charge to let us in. We told them we could tell them exactly which two seats they were and that if no-one had claimed them by the kick-off then they had to be ours but all to no avail. For the entire game we moped around the perimeter outside bickering and desperately trying to work out which set of fans was cheering the loudest and begging anyone who walked past with a walkie-talkie for a scoreflash. In the end it didn't seem to matter so much because Leeds had lost. I had really mixed feelings because I so desperately wanted them to win but not if I couldn't be in there to see it. God knows what would have happened to our marriage if they had beaten Wigan, I would never have heard the end of it.

Christine Jones

No Choice

One afternoon we were on our way to St Helens for the match and misjudged the amount of petrol left in the car. We'd just turned off the A580 into the estates that lead to Knowsley Road, past the big garage on the corner, when the car started jumping and missing. I realised with horror that we were about to run out and we were still about a couple of miles from the ground and about quarter-of-an-hour from kick-off. Eventually the car came to a shuddering halt in the middle of the road and we had a terrible dilemma. Did we run back to the garage and beg a can or worry about that later and belt to the ground? It wasn't even a tough decision, the four of us jumped out pushed the car into the pavement as best we could – which caused an immediate traffic jam – and spirited away in the direction of the ground. We figured that it was unlikely that the car was going to be nicked, even in that neighbourhood, because it was immobile anyway. I don't think there was any long debate, one of us just shouted, 'Let's go' and we were off in a manner in which the players themselves would have been proud.

Graham Armitage

Saltergate

As fans who never miss a game, home or away, you're always pleased when a new venue comes up that you can add to your list. In that way we are a bit like trainspotters. In 1989 we were delighted that the game with Sheffield was moved to Chesterfield football ground beneath the famous spire. The pitch seemed really narrow but the terracing where we were was close to the pitch and gave it a good atmosphere. I'll always remember that match because it marked the second coming of Mark Laurie, who had been sensational when he came over five years before and was man of the match when we won the John Player. We'd shown patchy form up to his return but as soon as he ran out to a tremendous reception, our defence seemed to be ten times better. We won that match easily and lost few others that year as we went on to finish runners-up but the revival started in the most unlikely place and was triggered by one of my all-time favourites.

Des Simpson

Emerald Isle

Dublin for the Charity Shield in '95 was a great one-off. The match wasn't up to much, especially after Vass got sent off after less than ten minutes, but Kempy got a try on his debut and we got the chance to see legend and former hero Hugh McGahan working at the club for the first time. I was devastated that we never did get to sign him as a player when, at his peak, he

Post-match handshakes at the Showground, Dublin, scene of the 1995 Charity Shield.

was one of the best in the world. It was a really relaxed trip – more of an excuse for a holiday really – and we treated it as an opportunity for a good laugh. We got a flight from Manchester and were amazed that in the queue at the checkout in front of us were Maurice Lindsay, Stuart Cummings and other officials. When we arrived we got a taxi to our guest house only to find when we arrived that there was a notice on the door saying that it was shut because the owner had popped out to do some shopping, such was the pace of life over there. With no alternative we had to wait at the nearest pub and spent the afternoon extolling the virtues of rugby league to a vaguely interested public bar who were far more concerned with explaining to us the significance and excitement surrounding the impending

Gaelic football final that weekend. It was like a cultural exchange and every time we went to the bar to order one drink they poured us a round because there is no such thing as not keeping up in Dublin. When we had got back to the hotel I put the telly on and saw the end of the Irish Horse of the Year Show live from the picturesque Showgrounds that our boys were due to play on the next afternoon and I remember thinking that I hoped that the ground staff had loads of shovels. After the game on the Sunday we went for a drink out in the centre of Dublin and bumped into the Leeds team wandering through the pedestrian area, with pints in their hands, also taking in the local sights.

Benjamin Scott

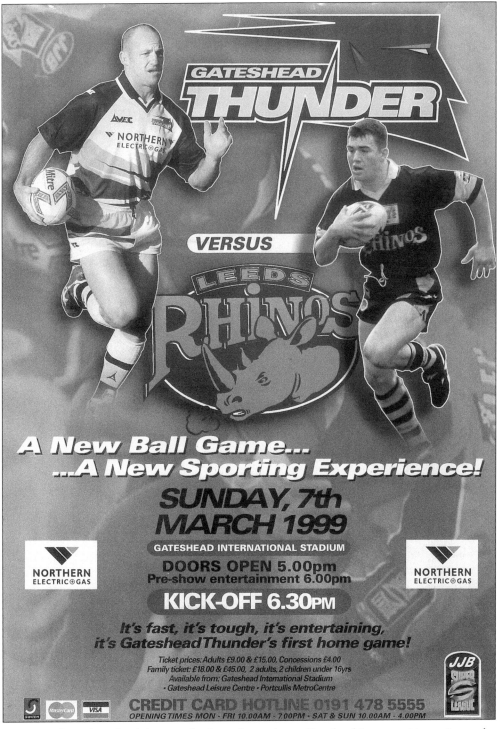

History in the making: Leeds become the first side to take on Gateshead in competitive action at the Thunderdome.

The intimidating bowl that is Odsal Stadium, Bradford.

Down T'Lane

I've always found camaraderie amongst league fans, even if they are rivals. Only last season I went to Castleford on my own and got in the queue for the turnstiles carrying a bag of sweets in my pocket. I got one out and started eating it and there were three home fans standing in front of me. One of them said, 'Is tha on tha own – well come and join us then'. They were as rough and as ready as you could imagine but hearts of gold. They took me in with them and no sooner had we got settled than another of them asked, 'Where's them sweets then?' To me that epitomises so much of the spirit that's contained within the game. They were great blokes, good to be with even though they were the opposition.

Gordon Morrish

CHAPTER 8

Laughter and Tears

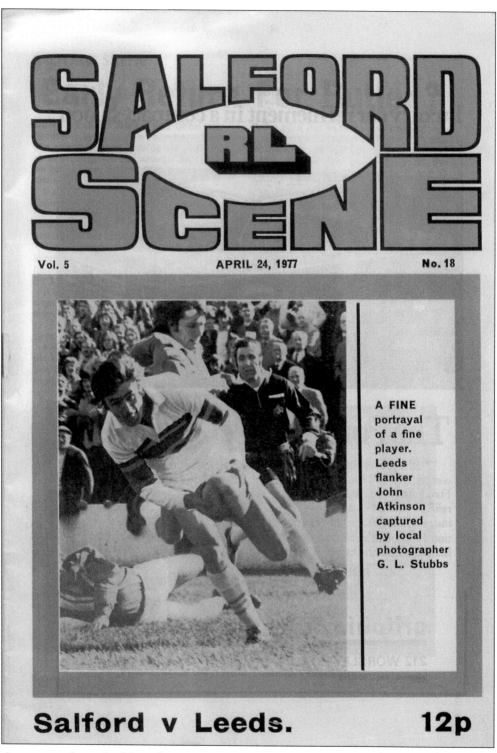

SALFORD RL SCENE

Vol. 5   APRIL 24, 1977   No. 18

A FINE portrayal of a fine player. Leeds flanker John Atkinson captured by local photographer G. L. Stubbs

Salford v Leeds.   12p

A programme from a fateful match.

Chris Sanderson

Late in the 1977 season, when Leeds had already qualified for Wembley, the final league match was at Salford. It was a beautiful sunny afternoon and I stayed at home to play with some friends in the garden while my dad went off to the match. I was really into rugby league at the time but you know what it's like when you're young and the prospect of running around and getting dirty is much more fun than sitting in a car on what seemed like a long journey. I knew that when he came home he'd give me a full report and a programme and I guess I thought that that was good enough. When he pulled into the drive again really early I could sense that something was wrong, especially as it looked like he had been crying. I ran up and asked him what had happened but he could barely bring himself to tell me. With a shaking voice he whispered that he had just witnessed a tragedy and like the rest of the crowd was in total shock. He had a clear view of Chris Sanderson making a tackle and he feared the worst when the game stopped immediately and there were frantic motions to the bench and the crowd went completely hushed. He could see medical staff shaking their heads and a stretcher being called for as both sets of players wandered around, many with their heads in their hands. He said he knew that it was serious straight away as they rushed the stretcher from the pitch and into the dressing room with a blanket covering his prone body. The match continued for a while although the crowd were virtually silent. At half-time it was solemnly announced that the game had been abandoned because Chris had tragically died and everyone just stood around bewildered and helpless before moving off in silence. Three weeks later Leeds won at Wembley, as much for Chris as themselves I suspect.

Steve Marshall

Behind Before the Start

Hull came to Headingley when they were at their pomp in the early eighties. For some reason the match started a bit early at two minutes to three. They kicked off and Andy Smith went to trap the ball but it bounced off his knee and into the arms of the on rushing John Muggleton who scored. Some of the fans were still coming into the ground and one, who saw the players out on the pitch and lining up, said to me 'Oh, have they started yet?' I had to break the news to him that we were already 5-0 down even though it wasn't yet three o'clock!

Ben Fenoughty

Where Am I?

Teddy Verrenkamp was playing on the wing for Leeds at Headingley and he got concussed. Nobody knew at the time and he went on to score six fabulous tries. He was absolutely brilliant, unstoppable, but when they came to ask him about them afterwards he couldn't remember a thing about any of them. It just must have been so instinctive.

Ruth Walker

Don't Tell the Doorman

When I first came out of the airforce about the age of twenty, we all used to meet up at the Headingley Pavilion for the big dance on a Saturday night – in fact that's where I met my future wife Shirley. It was such a popular venue, especially because there was a way to get in without paying. Quite a few of us used to shin up the drainpipe and through the window of the gents' toilets. It was a big social event in Leeds, and almost always all the players would be there after the game in the afternoon sporting black eyes and bruises. If it was a home match we'd go to the Oak or the Skyrack afterwards for a couple of beers first and then back for the dance. The bloke who ran the band there was called Cyril Mudd, a name you don't forget – they were very, very happy days.

Gordon Morrish

Too Much Spirit

The festive games were always something special anyway, but I'm sure that there have been matches on Boxing Day morning when some of the Leeds players have come out looking the worse for wear. Usually the odour that greets you as they run out is one of liniment but I'm sure for those games you could also detect the faint smell of rum. In the days before it all got as serious as it is now there was latitude for that kind of thing. Some of them used to use the fresh air and exercise as a hangover cure. Some I can think of from both sides used to try and get themselves sent off if they were clearly not feeling up to it before the days of substitutes being allowed. New Year's Day was the match that saw the fans suffering. There often used to be anything up to 20,000 or so in the ground but it was always subdued and quiet no matter who we were playing or how exciting it was. The applause was always polite because of the huge number of sore heads from the night before. Many is the time that a haze of whiskey fumes have hung over the main stand on those first of January afternoons.

Brian Davies

The Best Tackle of All

One of the most memorable tackles I have ever seen up close happened on a bright, sunny afternoon at Headingley. It was a pretty uneventful game between Leeds and Widnes, a team that was high on our most disliked list then. We were standing in our usual position in the Paddock, near the Leeds bench, as the players ran back out for the second half. One of the last to emerge was Craig Innes, our tough tackling Kiwi centre who was one of the best-looking in the side, who proceeded to throw up on the touchline having obviously had too much water in the dressing room during the break, in full view of us. It didn't seem to bother him too much, he just jogged on and took up his place but I remember thinking that that was all we needed, a team that tackles when it feels like it and a star player with food poisoning. The trainers did their best to cover the offending

One of the best promotional gimmicks ever – Mascot Ronnie the Rhino stands for Parliament in the 1997 General Election. He not only got over 140 votes but also became a question on *University Challenge*.

area with sand and the match kicked off again. Soon afterwards, Widnes centre Andy Currier, one of our least favourite players, ran towards us with the ball under his arm and heading for the line. Innes somehow appeared out of nowhere, pulled him to the floor by his ankles and slid him into touch unbelievably through the sandy mess he had created. We howled with laughter as he dusted himself down and had the perfect excuse to continue heckling him throughout the rest of the afternoon. It was worth the admission fee just to see his face when he got up and realised what had happened.

Lyn Belvedere

Wigan

One year we went to Wigan for a midweek night match and, to avoid the heavy traffic, came round the back way off the M62. Being unfamiliar with the route we got a bit lost and thought we would ask one of the locals the way to the ground. I was sat in the passenger seat and my dad was driving when he pulled up to the kerb, wound down the window and he leaned across to ask directions to Central Park. The guy, who was about middle-aged and casually dressed then proceeded to talk for a couple of minutes, interspersing his words with the odd gesticulation to the left or right. When we had thought that he had finished, Dad shouted 'Thanks' and I wound up the window as he pulled off. 'Get any of that?' he said to me, 'Not a word' I said, to which he replied 'No, me neither.' It went from bad to worse after that. Soon afterwards, on the same road, we came across a small garage and popped in to ask for directions. 'Oh you're on the right road here' said the attendant without batting an eyelid. Eventually after another couple of miles or so we came to Springfield Park, home of Wigan Athletic, which was completely locked and in total darkness as they weren't playing. Eventually we found the right ground ourselves but we did miss the kick-off.

Howard Brooks

Out of Position

In the days when second row forwards were not perceived to be the fittest and slickest and most mobile of men I can remember Phil Cookson starting a game for Leeds at Headingley on the wing. There was much hilarity in the ground and everybody started laughing when they read out the teamsheet over the Tannoy. We thought it must have been a mistake or a joke but there he was running out wearing the ill-fitting number five shirt – it was a really bizarre sight.

Sue Munden

A trademark try – Garry Schofield's interception against Featherstone at Elland Road in 1995 helped take Leeds back to Wembley.

The tightly packed ground of Wheldon Road, Castleford, always ensures Leeds players and fans receive a warm reception.

Oh No You're Not

Leeds had scraped into the Premiership and had somehow beaten Castleford at Wheldon Road in the last minute in the first round to set up a trip to Hull. We were the underdogs and the usual Boulevard welcome meant that we were pretty quiet as we sat in the new John Smiths stand, surrounded by black and white fans who were taunting us with their cries of 'What a waste of money' and the like. Unbelievably, we led going into the last minute and we were becoming a bit more boisterous ourselves at the prospect of another highly unlikely victory. I was so excited at the thought and in a state of glee grasped my husband's arm and shouted so that everyone around us could hear, 'I'm so excited, I've never been to a final before'. At that exact moment John Gallagher fumbled a high kick near the Leeds line and Hull scored to win. Hubby just turned and looked me straight in the eye and replied, 'And you never will, love'.

Lisa Parke

117

Mick Shoebottom
testimonial brochure

THE WHOLE OF THE REVENUE FROM THE SALE OF THIS BROCHURE WILL GO TO THE TESTIMONIAL FUND

T E N PENCE

Design/Production H Horsborough   Advertising R Armitage

A tribute to one of the finest players ever, whose career was tragically cut short in 1971.

118

Two for the Price of One

Matt Schultz was carried from the field at Widnes with ruptured knee ligaments. As he was being lowered into the dugout by Dean Riddle and physiotherapist Stuart Walker, someone distracted them and they banged his head on the top of the concrete bunker and broke his nose as well. At least it took the pain from his leg away.

Stuart Duffy

Getting Mouthy

The first time I stuck up for myself and the team was at St Helens. I was only about twelve and John Gallagher was disgracefully spear tackled by a couple of Saints players which amazingly went unpunished by the referee but caused the Leeds full-back to be taken off. As he was led past us with a neck brace on at the tunnel end of the ground and into the dressing rooms, a home fan near me started screaming that he was useless and another Leeds waste of money and so on. I just had to bite and ended up having a massive argument with him about them being a set of cheats. I've never looked back since and although the incident probably finished him as a rugby league player it was the making of me as a fan.

Andrew Jagger

Choice Remark

Unbelievably we won at Wigan in 1991 with a below strength team against their supposedly all-conquering superstars. There weren't many Leeds fans there that night because it was on satellite TV and it was going to be a question of how many we lost by. To win was sensational – especially as John Bentley scored a magnificent length-of-the-field try – but to nil them was mindblowing. We made the most of it, jigging and dancing on the terraces behind the posts at the far end and understandably getting totally carried away. As we were walking out by the chip van at the top of the steps, all chuffed, this bloke with a Wigan scarf on looked over and shouted, 'Oh yeah and what have you ever won?' Quick as a flash my mate turned round, looked him in the eye and answered, 'Maybe so but at least me wife doesn't look like a muppet'. We just howled, it seemed like the perfect remark for the occasion and has stuck in my mind ever since. We spent the entire journey home singing 'You've lost that Loving feeling' at the top of our voices in tribute to the Wigan fans.

Ryan Duckett

The Wake

One of the most depressing games to be at was the 1995 Premiership Final at Old Trafford when we were mercilessly tonked by Wigan by a record score. They had beaten us at Wembley the week before as well and to be honest we were dreading the return fixture. We

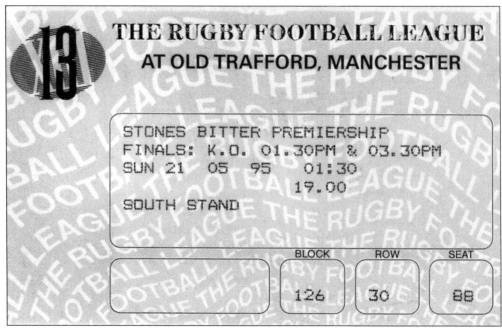

THE RUGBY FOOTBALL LEAGUE
AT OLD TRAFFORD, MANCHESTER

```
STONES BITTER PREMIERSHIP
FINALS: K.O. 01.30PM & 03.30PM
SUN 21  05  95   01:30
                 19.00
SOUTH STAND
```

	BLOCK	ROW	SEAT
	126	30	88

Ignominy! Leeds are humiliated by the mighty Wigan. Only self-deprecating humour got the fans through the afternoon.

felt we had a real chance in London but come the day we'd never really looked like winning and we were really down all that week following. I can't even imagine how the players must have felt. There were injuries to some of our best, including Hanley and Schofield, and we feared the worst. I don't think I've ever dreaded going to a game more, especially as the whole thing was being beamed live to the nation. Unfortunately our fears proved well-founded and Wigan began superbly and got better, shocking our usually vociferous support into near silence. In the midst of the despair, though, there is always someone who can raise a laugh. Late in the game, with Wigan already ahead by over sixty points, Leeds broke away and amazingly Craig Innes posted a try. We were so embarrassed by then that we were hardly in the mood for

celebration but someone behind me shouted out in frustration above the eerie silence, 'We effing needed that' which raised a smile. Then someone else called over, 'Come on Leeds you're cutting it a bit fine' which got us smirking before my mate joined in with, 'Heads up lads, only another fifty-eight drop goals to go!'

Garry Morrell

Quick Wit

They probably still do it a Wheldon Road, but when someone is read out on the Castleford teamsheet their name is accompanied by that of their personal sponsor. We were there on the popular side just after they had signed Lee Crooks from us in the late eighties

What the self-respecting
are buying at Harvey
Nichols these days!

and the man in the microphone started
off with, 'At number one…' and after
every name there was a loud cheer from
the home fans around us. When they
came to number eight, the announcer
shouted, 'Lee Crooks, sponsored by' and
before he could get the words out a huge
Leeds fan at the back of the stand
bellowed at the top of his voice,
'Tetley's bitter' which had us all in
stitches.

Phil Smithson

Few Words

We were getting our usual
disgraceful hiding at Wigan and I
was standing outside the dressing room
at half-time. Coach Douggie Laughton
walked in, left the door open, said, 'I
think we can do better than that lads in
the second half', turned round and left.
That was it, short and to the point!

Stuart Duffy

Tales of the Unexpected

Of the multitude of matches I've
seen, two stand out because we
attended them more in hope or blind
faith than expectation. The first was the
infamous Challenge Cup quarter-final at
Wigan in 1947, a ground that we had
become accustomed to losing at – in

121

fact that could have applied to almost any venue in Lancashire. The occasion was one of the most tense and nerve-wracking imaginable and I'll never lose the potent vision of Dickie Williams' try and Bert Cook's incredible goal from the halfway line in ankle-deep mud and the delirium they brought. Those two cameo moments will live with me forever. By contrast, I can still recall a match on Boxing Day at Headingley when Leeds had Bob McMaster and twelve reserves lining up to face a renowned Wakefield Trinity outfit and amazingly won. The atmosphere was sensational as the underdogs bearing our colours rose so gallantly to the occasion for an unbelievable victory against all the odds.

Neil Jeffries

Too Nervous

I can't watch Leeds when they're on the telly. If they go behind I haven't got the guts to stay in the room and see if they can get back into the game. If you're there you can get more of a feel for how they're playing or what is happening outside the narrow picture. It's too easy when you're at home just to go into another room or out in the garden and brood. You feel as though you can't help in any way when you are so isolated and I just hate it when they lose.

Jim Munden

Raison d'Être

One of my most shameful episodes of support would undoubtedly be after Mick Shoebottom got clattered in the injury that ended his career. For the next two years after we played Salford they, and the players we held responsible, came in for some horrendous abuse. I actually missed the game it occurred in because I had tonsillitis but I can vividly remember seeing it on television at the time because it was featured on the BBC. My dad and brother saw it live and they said at the time it looked really bad and, of course, it was. There is this great wave of emotion surrounding following your team, all the things you go through from being brought along as a kid, keeping the scrapbooks all the specific smells and sounds that trigger memories. These are things that make you then go on, when you end up living somewhere like Worcester, to want to set up your own club and spread the word irrespective of whether the place is a wasteland so far as Rugby League is concerned. If you didn't have this great reservoir of memories and very strong feelings inside you that stay with you then you wouldn't put up with all the obstacles and grief and people thinking that you're barmy. I guess that its because of the passion, the traditions and the experiences that we all become evangelists. It's a personality disorder that we're stuck with – you can't do anything about it. You know it's the best game in the world so you keep going.

Andy Cave

Out to enthrall and capture the next generation of fans, who mob their newly found heroes.

Real Hard Men

Derek Hallas tells the story of when Leeds played at Hull in the early sixties and, like it always has been, the Boulevard was a pretty intimidating place. Hull had a renowned pack – Harry Markham, Ted and Bill Drake, Tommy Harris, Mick Scott and one of the best loose forwards of all time Johnny Whiteley – some of the toughest and most fearsome men around. Early in the game, Hull hooker Tommy Harris went down injured in a fair tackle, his ankle had gone, and he had to be helped from the field. In those days there were no substitutes and scrums were contested so it looked like a big blow for the Airlie Birds as Leeds would be almost assured constant possession. Just as the visiting players were thinking victory would be theirs, a scrum formed as Harris had dropped the ball when he fell. As soon as it had packed down, Leeds hooker Bernard Prior's head came flying out with blood pouring from his rearranged nose and he was led from the field. Just over the roar of the crowd, Mick Scott's voice could be heard on the pitch. 'Looks like it's twelve a side now' he scowled in a Hull accent.

Stuart Duffy

123

Word in Your Ear

The opposition kicker put up a huge bomb during an 'A' team game at Headingley. Just as Leeds full back Lee Maher was in the process of leaping to catch it a voice boomed out on the tannoy 'Don't let that ball bounce!'. Timekeeper Billy Watts was inadvertently leaning on the microphone button at the time and his pleading cry caused all on the pitch and in the stands to freeze for what was a split second but felt like a few minutes. Needless to say, in the shock and surprise the ball did indeed hit the deck.

Ben Fenoughty

Misled

It's probably apocryphal because memory plays tricks, but I seem to remember sitting in the back of my dad's car on the way to somewhere like Workington or Barrow many years ago when I was a youngster. He hadn't been up there for several seasons and the road layout had probably changed anyway. As we approached the town centre there was uncertainty as to the way to the ground and all the usual landmarks seemed to have gone astray. We looked round for clues or road signs and weren't having much success when he spied a car in front with a sticker in the back window supporting the home side. 'We'll follow them' he said, 'They must know where they're going'. The bloke in front must have thought that we were mad as we risked running red lights and other traffic just to stay behind him. Alternately Dad was saying, 'Yes, I think I recognise this bit' or 'I'm not sure if this guy knows a short cut but I can't see a crowd.' Eventually the car in front started meandering through some country lanes and into a small village on the edge of town before disappearing into his drive at high speed. We sheepishly drove straight past, trying to avoid his undoubted glare, totally lost and miles from the match. Not surprisingly he didn't invite us in for lunch.

Benjamin Scott

Differentials

We had a good friend who married former Leeds player Gareth Price. He had a newsagents in Headingley after he retired from the game and we were in the same trade so we used to meet up with him every now and again. Gareth always used to enjoy talking about his rugby experiences and being such a keen fan we were equally as eager to listen. During his time, the forwards always used to get paid less than the backs but one of the fastest men on the team was Ike Owens who played loose forward and went on to represent Great Britain. He asked to go in front of the committee after a while and demanded to be reclassified as a back, because he was not only as quick as them but he did a damn sight more running. In fact, because of the overall graft that he did, he reckoned that he should be paid as a back and a forward.

Gordon Morrish

The long, nervous wait for the gates to open at Wembley.

The obligatory war paint for today's avid army of fans.

Radio Star

I became something of a regular caller on Radio Headingley, the club's matchday radio station, for a while. There was one occasion when I was flying back from Heathrow to Leeds for a Friday night match at Headingley when I thought I would ring through and get the latest team news and gossip. As usually happened, I got involved in some debate or other about the state of the game or the way the team were playing and completely ignored all the announcements coming over the tannoy in the terminal. Not surprisingly, whilst I was in the middle of the broadcast, my flight left without me and I hurriedly had to find a hotel in London to watch the game on television. There was a compensation, though. Soon after the end of another match when we used to ring in with our opinion of the night's action, I heard presenter Stuart Duffy say, 'And after the break we'll be getting the thoughts of coach Dean Bell, prop Neil Harmon and Richard Stevens.' It did sound strange and gratifying to be listed in such illustrious company.

Richard Stevens

Second Time Around

We went to Wembley in 1994 and stopped at a pub on the way back in Leicester just off the motorway. The following year we did exactly the same, down to London, defeated in the cup

Here's to the next century of support.

final and back to this same pub. A local rugby union player from some village team in Leicestershire came up to me and said, 'Were you here around this time last year?' I looked at him a bit suspiciously just in case there was an unpaid round of drinks or we had broken some ornamental vase before admitting we had but why did he ask. He replied that he could remember getting very drunk with some people from Leeds but that was all and was it us. When I confirmed that it was we ended up having a repeat performance.

Michael Collins

Not a Dry Eye

When the Rhinos players brought the cup round to show us at Wembley, with all their children in tow, I was in floods of tears. I've cried a lot at Leeds matches in the past but this was a different kind of emotion, it was as much relief as ecstasy because all of a sudden we had actually won something, we were no longer under achievers – we were at that moment the best team in the game which is what I had followed them for so many years to be able to say. All of a sudden some of the ghosts of the past, matches and memories where we had fallen short or not lived up to our billing or the huge weight of expectation, had been exorcised. I remember thinking as we cheered and hugged and shouted at our current heroes that somehow the crossbar incident in 1982 at Swinton didn't feel so bad now – finally our day had come.

Sarah Gilmore

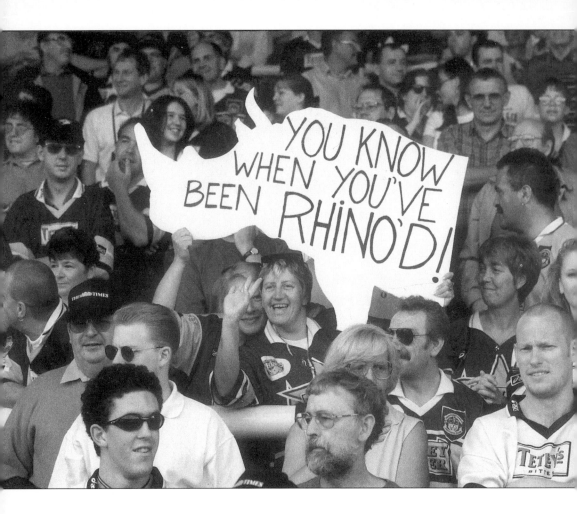

Epilogue

I've always said that a good bit of rugby, like some clever interpassing, is equal to a beautiful picture, a piece of music or a poem and that the men who conjure them up are true artists. I've moved heaven and earth to watch a match, I won't miss. There's a whole crowd of us who go together and they're all as daft as I am.

Ruth Walker